Diamonds in the Rough

The Best Golf in the West
for $35 or Less

Patrick J. Sanfilippo

FIRST EDITION

CIGRA PUBLICATIONS

Diamonds in the Rough
The Best Golf in the West for $35 or Less

Patrick J. Sanfilippo

FIRST EDITION
Published by CIGRA Publications
P.O. Box 50520
Sparks, Nevada 89435

ISBN: 0-9655632-3-5
Library of Congress Catalog Card #: 96-72239
Printed in the United States of America

Table of Contents

Acknowledgement

An endeavor such as this is never really a solo flight, and I am grateful to everyone who has helped. A big Sparks salute to the Mayor of B Street, William Abnah Hunt, for his encouragement and input right from the start. To Steve Simon, who has opened so many doors. To Scott Johnson for his invaluable assistance. To Dave Leech, whose propensity toward wagering, combined with a lack of expertise on the links, inadvertently helped finance this project. To the late Rich Mackenzie, who was, and continues to be, a great inspiration. You're not forgotten, Airman. To Mogo, Jr., Herman J. and Dean Parker. Finally, a special thanks to Karen, whose belief and support many years ago allowed this to happen—thanks KABES.

Cover Photograph: Steve Smith Photography, Eugene, Oregon
Editing: World Wide Words, Eugene, Oregon

Statement of Intent

Every effort has been made to ensure that the details, prices, addresses, phone numbers and directions herein are accurate as of January, 1997.

To maintain total objectivity, all visits to the golf courses listed herein were made without any prior arrangement. The intent to write a book or rate the course was never mentioned or implied. No compensation of any sort has been offered by or received from any golf course listed in this book.

It is the author's intention to provide readers with as comprehensive a guide to superior golf courses in the stated price range as possible, and every effort has been made to include every qualified course. If, however, the reader feels there have been omissions, or knows of a golf course that seems to meet the criteria of this book, we would appreciate any and all input. In fact, this input will be most welcome as we update future editions. All submissions will be carefully considered.

Additionally, we guarantee the satisfaction of our readers. If for any reason you are not satisfied, you may obtain a full refund by returning this book to GIGRA Publications, PO Box 50520, Sparks, NV 89435.

Introduction

The West is one of the world's most popular and highly regarded golf destinations—and rightly so. There's great weather, dramatic scenery and an abundance of courses in a remarkable variety of settings. When all these riches blended with the golf boom of the last decade the result was, and continues to be, a drastic increase in green fees.

In the major resort areas like Hawaii, Las Vegas, Phoenix/Scottsdale and the Monterey Peninsula, $100+ green fees have become the norm. Other areas in the West have seen courses in the $25-35 bracket shoot up to the $50-75 level in just a short time.

As green fees began to take more and more of our vacation and travel budgets, it became apparent that alternatives were necessary.

Enter "Diamonds in the Rough" —your personal guide to high quality, affordable golf in the West. It is a book that features over 160 wonderful courses in the seven state area of Arizona, California, Nevada, Oregon, Washington, Utah and Hawaii. These are courses with designs and settings as diverse as the West itself. All are $35 or less, with the majority in the mid-20s, and all offering an excellent alternative to their high-priced neighbors.

Compiling this guide has been a three year labor of love involving the inspection of over 400 courses. It is not a listing of the lowest priced courses in each area, but rather a selection of the very best each area has to offer using the following criteria:

- A maximum green fee of $35 (the average is $24)
- Full-size 18-hole layouts with par of 70-73. (There are some special exceptions which are noted in their sections)
- Desirability of location and course setting
- Above average course design and maintenance
- Level of clubhouse facilities and amenities

Additionally, all course inspections were unannounced and all green fees were paid by the author. No financial or other considerations were involved. The best of these courses are designated "Eagle Award" winners. These are the cream of the crop, and represent the finest in affordable public golf. In fact, these courses represent good value even at twice their rate!

Ultimately, this book is a celebration of discovery—discovery of truly great golfing experiences at bargain prices—of hidden jewels in unforgettable settings. And in some of the finest resort and vacation areas in the world, you'll never pay more than $35!

As a lifelong golfer and native of the West, I invite you to share these Diamonds in the Rough. Enjoy as many as you can.

"Love and putting are mysteries for the philosophers to solve. Both subjects are beyond golfers."

Tommy Armour

CHAPTER 1

Arizona

Arizona *is* the West. Two of its borders are the Grand Canyon and the Colorado River. Its history is filled with stories about characters and places that have now become legendary.

But, it's sheer beauty and diversity are the most striking. With its breathtaking mixture of deserts and canyons and mountains and cliffs, the state offers an outstanding variety of settings; one more spectacular then the other, and its golf courses reflect that beauty and variety.

We have selected a wonderful group of courses located throughout the state that represent the finest in quality, affordable golf available to the public. You can play year-round in Arizona—just not in the same region. In the northern, mountain areas early spring through mid-fall is best, while in the southern desert areas fall through spring is ideal.

This chapter is divided into two sections, with the first covering the Phoenix-Tucson corridor, while the second covers the rest of the state. No matter where you wander, you're not far from excellent golf.

Arizona Quick Check

⓬	ANTELOPE HILLS	520-776-7888
❻	ARTHUR PACK	520-744-3322
⓫	BEAVER CREEK	520-567-4487
⓭	CERBAT CLIFFS	520-753-6593
❹	DOBSON RANCH	602-644-2291
❿	ELDEN HILLS	520-527-7999
❺	ELOY-TOHONO	520-466-7734
⓮	EMERALD CANYON	520-667-3366
❷	ENCANTO PARK	602-253-3963
❻	FRED ENKE	520-296-8607
❸	KEN MCDONALD	602-350-5250
❼	KINO SPRINGS	520-287-8701
⓯	MESA DEL SOL	520-342-1283
❷	PAPAGO	602-275-8428
❽	PUEBLO DEL SOL	520-378-6444
❻	RANDOLPH PARK	520-325-2811
❾	SILVER CREEK	520-537-2744
❶	TPC OF SCOTTSDALE	602-585-3939

REMINDER:
Except where noted, all courses are regulation size (6000+ yards), 18 hole, par 70-73 layouts with an average green fee of $24. Current maximum fee is noted next to course phone number.

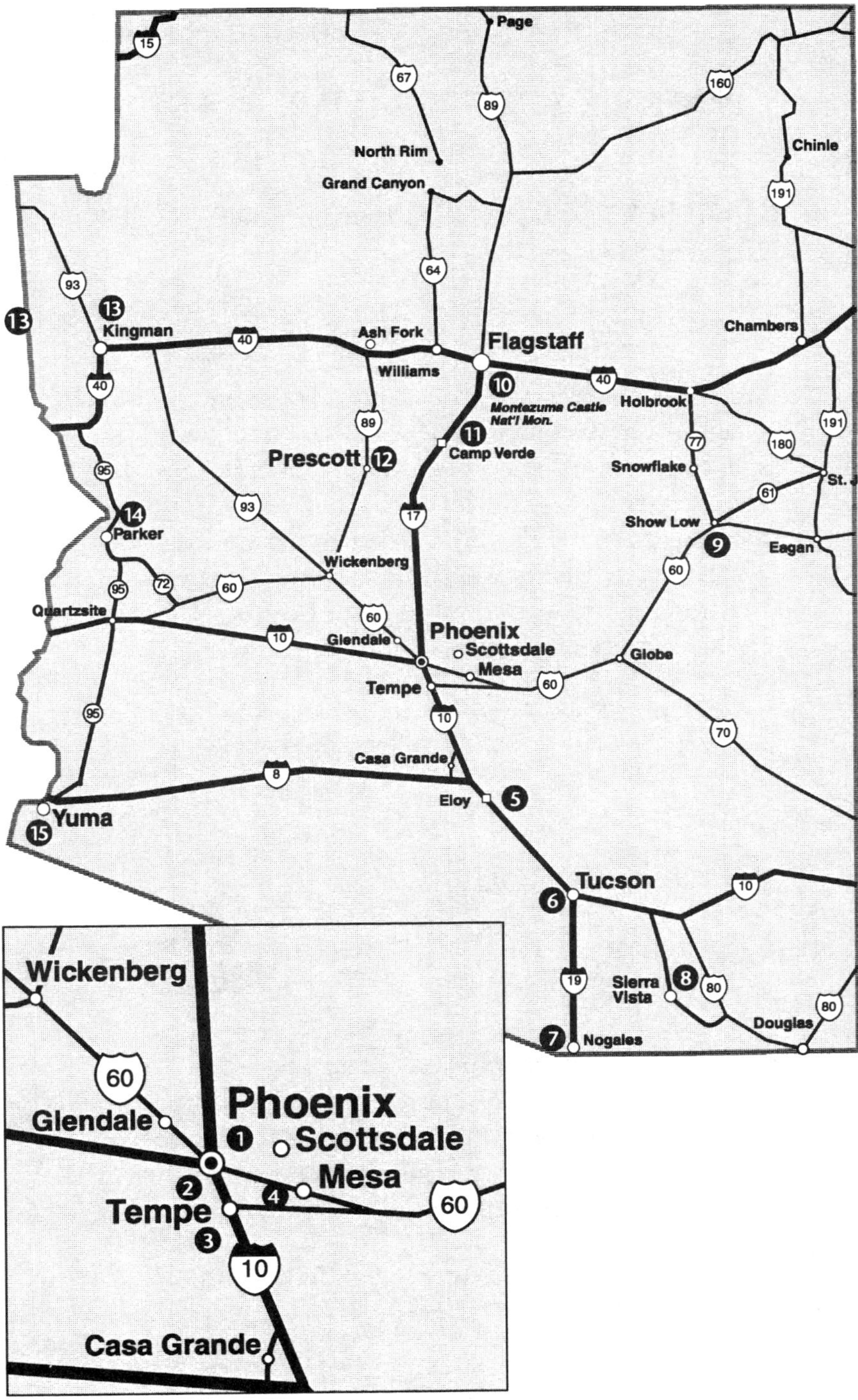

Page
North Rim
Grand Canyon
Chinle
13
Kingman
Ash Fork
Flagstaff
Williams
Chambers
10
Montezuma Castle Nat'l Mon.
Holbrook
11
Camp Verde
Prescott
12
Snowflake
St. Johns
14
Parker
Show Low
9
Eagan
Wickenberg
Quartzsite
Phoenix
Glendale
Scottsdale
Mesa
Tempe
Globe
Casa Grande
Eloy
5
Yuma
15
Tucson
6
Sierra Vista
8
Douglas
7
Nogales
Wickenberg
Phoenix
Glendale
1
Scottsdale
Mesa
2
4
Tempe
3
Casa Grande

— PHOENIX-SCOTTSDALE-TUCSON —

TPC OF SCOTTSDALE (Desert course)

17020 North Hayden
Scottsdale, AZ 85255
602-585-3939 $24

We start this chapter with the epitome of a diamond in the rough—The Desert Course at TPC. Great location (this 36 hole facility plays host to the Phoenix Open), wonderful setting, highest level of maintenance and a challenging Tom Weiskopf/Jay Morrish design for under $30. The City of Scottsdale is to be saluted for providing first-rate, affordable golf in a town that is otherwise extremely pricey.

Directions: Take Pima Road north past Frank Lloyd Wright and turn left at Bell Road into the course.

PAPAGO GOLF COURSE

5595 East Moreland
Phoenix, AZ 85008
602-275-8428 $26

Massive boulder outcroppings serve as a backdrop for this heavily treed, lengthy championship layout in Papago Park. Bring your "A" game and several extra balls. This is one of the top municipal courses in the state. Great challenge, super value.

Directions: Take McDowell Rd to 52nd. Turn south to Moreland and course on your left.

ENCANTO PARK GOLF COURSE

2705 N. 15th Ave.
Phoenix, AZ 85007
602-253-3963 $26

Not quite the challenge of Papago, but a very pleasant urban course in a parkland setting that contrasts the highrise skyline of nearby downtown Phoenix. Solid, straightforward track in good condition and under $30.

Directions: From I-17 take Thomas Road (Exit 201) and head east to 15th Ave. Turn right and follow to course on your left.

KEN MCDONALD GOLF COURSE

800 Divot Dr.
Tempe, AZ 85283
602-350-5250 $19

Mid-length, traditional "locals" course with trees and water coming into play on both the front and back nines. The course is in good condition, and with fees under $20 it is one of the best bargains in the Phoenix area.

Directions: Take Hwy 60 (Superstition Freeway) to Rural Rd. Exit 174). South on Rural to Divot Dr. Turn right and follow to course.

DOBSON RANCH GOLF COURSE

2155 So Dobson Rd
Mesa, AZ 85202
602-644-2291 $22

Well-maintained, well-run local course in suburban Mesa. Very playable, traditional layout with large greens and enough interesting holes to keep your attention. Comfortable setting, nice clubhouse.

Directions: Take Hwy 60 (Superstition Freeway) to Dobson Road (Exit 177) and head south to course on your left.

ELOY-TOHONO GOLF COURSE

Toltec Road and I-10
Eloy, AZ
520-466-7734 $24

This newer course is located halfway between Phoenix and Tucson, not far from Casa Grande. A long (more than 7000 yds from the tips) rolling, links-style layout heavily mounded and in excellent condition. A pleasant and inexpensive alternative that can be testy, particularly in the wind.

Directions: From I-10 in Eloy take Toltec Rd. (Exit 203) east and follow to course.

RANDOLPH PARK GOLF COURSE

600 S. Alvernon Way
Tucson, AZ 85711
520-325-2811 $22

This is a 36-hole facility located in the heart of Tucson. Randolph North is a current stop on the LPGA Tour and has hosted the PGA's Tucson Open. It is a long, scenic course, traditional in design, with tall trees and several water hazards. This championship layout is your best bet in the Tucson area. The other course, Dell Urich Municipal, has recently been refurbished and provides a less difficult alternative to the lengthy North course. Easily walkable and in excellent condition, this is a much improved version of the old Randolph South.

Directions: From I-10 take Speedway or Broadway exit and head east to Alvernon. Turn right and follow to course.

FRED ENKE GOLF COURSE

8251 E. Irvington
Tucson, AZ 85730
520-296-8607 $20

If you want a different type of challenge, you'll find it here. Difficult, limited-turf, target golf in the desert with vast areas of cactus and sagebrush separating tee boxes and landing pads. On this course, shot placement is critical. Beautiful, rugged Western setting and another of Tucson's fine "munis" under $30.

Directions: From I-10 take Broadway or Speedway exit to Kolb Rd. turn south. Continue on Kolb to Irvington Rd. and turn left to course (approximately 2 miles). From south of Tucson on I-10 take Kolb Rd exit and continue north to Irvington. Turn right and follow to course.

ARTHUR PACK DESERT GOLF COURSE

9101 N. Thornydale Rd
Tucson. AZ 85741
520-744-3322 $21

Lee Trevino had a hand in the design of this solid, traditional layout just north of town. Not an extremely difficult course, but water does come into play on several holes. The greens are in great shape, and the general condition of the course is good. Nice staff, nice setting.

Directions: Take I-10 to Ina Rd. exit. Go east on Ina to Thornydale Rd. and turn left to course.

— ROAMING ARIZONA —

KINO SPRINGS GOLF COURSE

1 Kino Springs Dr.
Nogales, AZ 85621
520-287-8701 $22

Rambling, rural desert course a few miles east of Nogales. Well-maintained, mid-length layout in a comfortable and relaxed setting. Your best bet in the Nogales area.

Directions: From I-19 in Nogales take Hwy 82 six miles to course on your right.

PUEBLO DEL SOL GOLF COURSE

2770 St. Andrews
Sierra Vista, AZ 85635
520-378-6444 $26

As close as you can get to country club golf without paying membership fees. Long, challenging championship course with narrow fairways and excellent, but extremely fast, greens. Set in a valley surrounded by mountain vistas, the course is in immaculate condition and easily walkable. Upscale clubhouse, great staff and the best value in Southern Arizona.

Directions: From I-10 take Hwy 90 south to Sierra Vista. From there take Hwy 92 south of town to St. Andrews Dr. Turn right and follow to course.

SILVER CREEK GOLF CLUB

2051 Silver Lake Blvd.
Show Low, AZ 85901
520-537-2744 $35

Located in the White Mountain Lake area not far from Show Low, this beautifully maintained resort course is one of the best public facilities in Northern Arizona. Links-style layout with four sets of tees provide challenge for all levels. Marvelous mountain hideaway. First-class operation throughout. Definitely worth a trip. Mid-April thru mid-October is the best time to play this jewel.

Directions: From Hwy 77 in Show Low take Hwy 60 east five miles to Bourdon Ranch Rd. Turn left (north) and follow to course approximately 7 miles.

ELDEN HILLS GOLF COURSE

2380 N. Oakmont Dr.
Flagstaff, AZ 86004
520-527-7999 $25

Semi-private resort club in good condition, located at the gateway to the Grand Canyon. Not long but rolling and sometimes hilly layout is heavily treed and very scenic. Top-notch clubhouse operation that has a "members" feel about it. Course is open year-round, but winter play is sporadic due to weather. Spring thru fall is best.

Directions: From I-40 take Country Club Dr. exit and head south 1/2 mile to Oakmont Dr. Turn right and follow to course.

BEAVER CREEK GOLF CLUB

Lakeshore Dr.
Lake Montezuma, AZ 86342
520-567-4487 $31

This place is comfortable, rural and rustic. Straight-ahead golf off the beaten path in scenic mountain surroundings. Course maintenance and clubhouse operations are both above average. Open year-round, but best times would be spring thru fall.

Directions: From I-17 take exit 193 and head east approximately 3 miles. Follow signs to course

ANTELOPE HILLS GOLF COURSES

1 Perkins Dr.
Presscot, AZ 86301
520-776-7888 $32

Full-service mountain resort 90 miles north of Phoenix and not far from Sedona, providing two completely different 18 hole layouts. The North course is a more traditional design with narrow fairways, mature trees and tough greens. It is the higher rated of the two. The newer South course is an open links-style design, with most of the trouble coming around the greens. A good short game is vital. Both courses are in excellent condition. Nice setting, good clubhouse, a well-run operation. Courses are open year-round, but winter can be hit and miss at this elevation— 5300 feet. Late spring to early fall is ideal.

Directions: Seven miles north of Prescott off Hwy 89. Course is on your right.

CERBAT CLIFFS GOLF COURSE

1001 Gates Ave.
Kingman, AZ 86401
520-753-6593 $22

Enjoyable, affordable high-desert golf. Formerly Kingman Muni, the course has been expanded to 18 holes and upgraded throughout. It is now in very good condition. Pleasant, walkable layout with some easy holes and some very difficult holes in a natural Northwest Arizona setting of plateaus and dramatic cliffs. You'll be hearing more about this place.

Directions: From I-40 take Stockton Hill Rd. exit and head south to Gates. Turn right and follow to course.

EMERALD CANYON GOLF COURSE

72 Emerald Canyon Dr.
Parker, AZ 85344
520-667-3366 $28

This is a unique desert course set in a canyon, surrounded by cliffs next to the Colorado River. The view from the 17th tee box is extraordinary; one of the most dramatic vistas in the state. The course is tricky and challenging. It can be particularly difficult the first time around. Good course maintenance. Exceptional value. This facility is open year-round, but summers can be hot.

Directions: 7 miles north of Parker off Hwy 95. Course is on your left.

MESA DEL SOL GOLF COURSE

10583 Camino del Sol
Yuma, AZ 85365
520-342-1283 $28

Very nice semi-private course, located outside of Yuma in an upscale subdivision. Traditional, fairly flat layout in a relaxing desert setting with red rock cliffs in the background. Your best bet in this area.

Directions: From I-8 about 10 miles east of Yuma take Exit 12 (Fortuna Rd) and head north to N. Frontage road which parallels the freeway. Turn right on N. Frontage and continue to Camino del Sol. Turn left and follow to course.

CHAPTER 2

California

The Golden State is indeed a gold mine of golfing greatness. Every type of terrain, every type of course, every type of weather can be found in the mountains, forests, shores and deserts of California. Like the song says, "This could be heaven or this could be hell." We think we've found some slices of heaven.

Because the state is so big, and so diverse, we have divided it into five sections, each of which will be treated like a separate chapter with its own map and quick-check. We start with Northern California.

This area runs from the Oregon border to the San Francisco Bay Area. It features a splendid selection of exceptional courses in a variety of settings. From the Pacific Ocean to Mount Shasta; from urban to remote; from the wine country of Napa Valley to the foothills of the High Sierras, you'll find a wonderful assortment of mostly traditional courses. With the exception of a few of the mountain courses, the mild climate of Northern California will allow you to play comfortably year-round.

Northern California Quick Check

6	ANCIL HOFFMAN	916-482-5660
1	BEAU PRE	707-839-2342
10	BENNET VALLEY	707-528-3673
7	DRY CREEK RANCH	209-745-2330
3	FALL RIVER VALLEY	916-336-5555
4	GRAEAGLE MEADOWS	916-836-2323
12	HARDING PARK	415-664-4690
12	LINCOLN PARK	415-221-9911
2	MOUNT SHASTA	916-926-3052
9	NAPA MUNI	707-255-4333
10	OAKMONT	707-539-0415
8	PARADISE VALLEY	707-426-1600
13	SHARP PARK	415-355-8546
11	TILDEN PARK	510-848-7373
5	WOODCREEK	916-771-4653

REMINDER:
Except where noted, all courses are regulation size (6000+ yards), 18 hole, par 70-73 layouts with an average green fee of $24. Current maximum fee is noted next to course phone number.

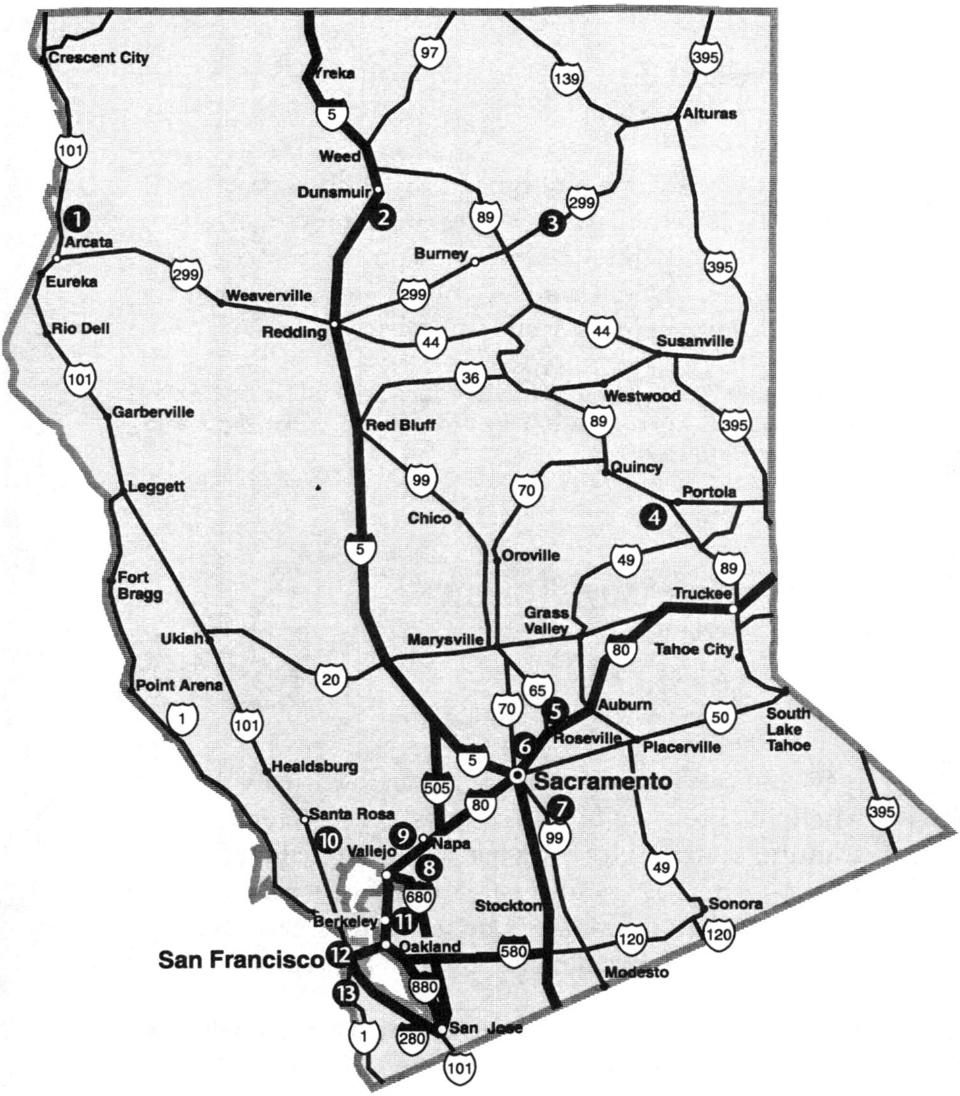

Crescent City
Yreka
97
139
395
5
Alturas
101
Weed
Dunsmuir
1
2
89
3
299
Arcata
Burney
Eureka
299
395
Weaverville
299
Redding
Rio Dell
44
44
Susanville
101
36
Westwood
Garberville
Red Bluff
89
395
Quincy
99
70
Portola
Leggett
Chico
4
5
Oroville
49
89
Fort Bragg
Truckee
Grass Valley
Ukiah
Marysville
80
Tahoe City
20
65
Point Arena
70
5
Auburn
1
101
50
South Lake Tahoe
6
Roseville
Placerville
Healdsburg
5
Sacramento
505
80
7
395
Santa Rosa
10
9
Vallejo
Napa
99
8
49
680
Stockton
Sonora
Berkeley
11
120
120
Oakland
San Francisco
12
580
Modesto
880
13
280
San Jose
1
101

BEAU PRE GOLF CLUB

1777 Norton Rd.
McKinlyville, CA 95519
707-839-2342 $20

Far up the coast north of Eureka you'll discover an oceanside jewel of a course. The short, unique layout features heavily tree-lined fairways and some exciting ocean views. Overall maintenance is very good, and the setting is idyllic. Just a wonderful place.

Directions: From Hwy 101 take Murray Rd. exit to Central Ave and turn north. Follow to Norton Rd. Turn right and follow to course.

MOUNT SHASTA RESORT

1000 Siskiyou Lake Blvd.
Mt. Shasta, CA 96067
916-926-3052 $20

New, full-service resort course just below the overwhelming presence of Mount Shasta, in a serene yet stunning setting. Not long but well-designed and well-maintained with a country club feel. Great place to be. Accommodations on-site. Due to winter weather, best time to play here would be May thru September.

Directions: From I-5 take Central Mount Shasta exit and head west. Follow signs to resort (just off W.A. Barr Rd.).

FALL RIVER VALLEY GC

42889 Hwy 299 E.
Fall River Mills, CA 96028
916-336-5555 $24

The key word here is long. How long? Well, the course plays 7365 yds from the tips and 6832 from the whites. The longest hole in the state is here: a 666 yd par 5 and 400+ yd par 4s are everywhere. Located in a valley between Mt. Shasta and Mt. Lassen National Park, this highly rated, well-maintained course is as "out there" as you can get. Forget trying to score; just enjoy the magnificent surroundings. Course is open spring through fall.

Directions: From I-5 in Redding take Hwy 299 and head east approximately 70 miles. Course is on your right just West of town. From Mt. Shasta take Hwy 89 south to Hwy 299. Head east to the course.

GRAEAGLE MEADOWS GOLF CLUB

Highway 89
Graeagle, CA 96103
916-836-2323 $32

Set in a meadow among the pines of Plumas National Forest, this gorgeous mountain hideaway is one of the prettiest in Northern California. The layout is long and well-planned, offering a good variety of holes. A great escape in the Sierras that is well worth a trip. Course is best played May through October.

Directions: From I-80 in Truckee take Hwy 89 east approximately 50 miles to course on your right. From Reno, NV take 395 north to 70 east to Blairsden (Hwy 89). Turn left and follow to course on your left. Total time from Reno is one hour.

WOODCREEK GOLF CLUB

5880 Woodcreek Oaks Blvd.
Roseville, CA 95747
916-771-GOLF $27

A remarkable new facility in the Sierra foothills just outside of Sacramento. Created in the suburbs by Robert Muir Graves, this rolling, traditional layout features hundreds of oak trees, lots of water and bunkers everywhere. An extremely well-designed course with a mature, comfortable feel about it despite its newness. Top-notch clubhouse, pro shop and practice area. A genuine diamond in the rough and your best bet in the Sacramento area.

Directions: From I-80 take Riverside exit and head west on Cirby Way to Foothills. Turn right and continue on Foothills for 3 miles to Pleasant Grove Rd. Turn left and go to Woodcreek Oaks Blvd. Turn right and follow to course.

ANCIL HOFFMAN GOLF COURSE

6700 Tarshes Dr.
Carmichael, CA 95608
916-482-5660 $24

This established course has long been recognized as one of the best in the area. Its beautiful setting next to the American River and a demanding layout have contributed to that reputation. This is a very good course, and with a bit more attention to maintenance it could return to its proper status as a great course. Worth a play if you're in Sacremento.

Directions: From Business 80 take Marconi Ave exit and head east 5 miles to Fair Oaks Blvd. Turn right and follow to Van Alstine. Turn left and follow signs to course.

DRY CREEK RANCH GC

809 Crystal Way
Galt, CA 95632
209-745-2330 $26

Located some 20 miles south of Sacramento this "sleeper" is consistently rated as one of the best public courses in Northern California. Mid-length layout with several old oak trees and well-bunkered, small, slick greens. If you have a good score going into 18, play it safe on that hole. You'll save your score and your sanity. Good staff, nice clubhouse, definitely worth a trip.

Directions: From Hwy 99 take Central Galt exit and head east on C Street to Crystal Way. Turn right and follow to course.

PARADISE VALLEY GOLF COURSE

3950 Paradise Valley Dr
Fairfield, CA 94533
707-426-1600 $32

A convincing example of how good a municipal facility can be. This easily walkable Robert Muir Graves design plays tough from the whites and real tough from the tips with wind adding to the difficulty. As with most Graves layouts, water and sand bunkers are everywhere. A solid course with an exceptional finishing hole. Good driving range and a clubhouse and pro shop that project a suburban country-club atmosphere. Excellent all-around operation. Less than an hour from SF and worth the trip.

Directions: From I-80 take North Texas St exit. Turn right on NorthTexas to Dixon Hill. Turn left and on to Dover St. Turn left and follow to course.

NAPA MUNICIPAL GOLF COURSE

(Kennedy Park)
2295 Streblow Lane
Napa, CA 94558
707-255-4333 $25

Tough test for all levels in the Napa Valley. Water comes into play on most holes of this well-designed layout. Not a championship course but one that requires a variety of shots to score well. Great value in an otherwise expensive golf area.

Directions: Take Hwy 29 to Streblow Dr. in Napa, turn west at Streblow and follow to course.

OAKMONT GOLF CLUB WEST

7025 Oakmont Dr.
Santa Rosa, CA 95409
707-539-0415 $32

EAGLE AWARD

Wonderful country golf located between Santa Rosa and Sonoma. Beautifully maintained, traditional layout with mature oak trees protecting the fairways and some very "three-puttable" greens. This quality facility is an extraordinary value and your best bet in the Wine Country.

Directions: From Santa Rosa or Sonoma take Hwy 12 to Oakmont Dr. Turn west and follow to course.

BENNETT VALLEY GOLF COURSE

3330 Yulupa Ave.
Santa Rosa, CA 95405
707-528-3673 $20

As pleasant and enjoyable a round of golf as you could want. Instant comfort level from the moment you drive in. Not overly challenging but well maintained. Great setting, great greens, great course.

Directions: From Hwy 101 take Hwy 12 east to Bennet Valley Rd. and follow to course.

TILDEN PARK GOLF COURSE

Grizzley Peak @ Shasta Rd.
Berkeley, CA 94708
510-848-7373 $25

Scenic park-like setting above the University of California in the Berkeley hills. Mature, hilly, traditional layout that is not very forgiving. Miss a fairway here and you may never be heard from again. A beautiful place to play a round and your best bet in the East Bay.

Directions: From I-580 take Hwy 24 in Berkeley and exit on Fish Ranch Rd. Go north to Grizzly Peak and follow to course.

LINCOLN PARK GOLF COURSE

3139 Clement St.
San Francisco, CA 94121
415-221-9911 $25

Long time San Francisco favorite located "out in the Avenues" in a residential district removed from the commotion of the city. This very short (Par 68) layout challenges your accuracy and short game with its tight fairways and small greens. But the setting is what this course is all about. The views of the Pacific Ocean and the Golden Gate Bridge are something you will never forget.

Directions: From 19th Ave. turn west on Clement and follow to course.

HARDING PARK GOLF COURSE

Skyline Blvd @ Harding Rd.
San Francisco, CA 94132
415-664-4690 $30

Ken Venturi, George Archer and Johnny Miller grew up playing this former PGA Tour site located next to the Olympic Club. Excellent layout among the trees at Lake Merced offers a nostalgic, challenging golf experience. If the maintenance equaled the setting and design, this course would be an "Eagle Award" winner. Still, your best bet in San Francisco.

Directions: From 19th Ave. take Skyline Blvd. (Hwy 35) and head west to the course.

SHARP PARK GOLF COURSE

Highway 1 @ Sharp Park Rd.
Pacifica, CA 94044
415-355-8546 $25

Cruise down the coast on Hwy 1 a few miles south of San Francisco, and you'll discover a delightful Alister MacKenzie course. This master designer takes you through woods and forest on the front nine and then finishes along the coast. Starting times easier to get here than at Harding or Lincoln. When the sun is shining, this place is heaven.

Directions: From San Francisco take Hwy 1 south to Pacifica. Take Fairway Dr. exit to course.

CHAPTER TWO, PART 2

The Central Coast & Ventura County

Exciting, breathtaking, natural beauty from Monterey Bay to Santa Barbara. This is the Central Coast of California. As spectacular a mix of beaches, cliffs, mountains and rolling countryside as you'll ever see. And, the quality of golf rivals Mother Nature in its greatness. Eleven wonderful courses, five of them "Eagle Award" winners, make this a true golf heaven.

Central Coast and Ventura County Quick Check

❺ AVILA BEACH	805-595-2307
❶ DE LEVEAGA	408-423-7214
❾ ELKINS RANCH	805-524-1440
❹ MORRO BAY	805-772-4341
❷ PACIFIC GROVE	408-648-3175
❸ PASO ROBLES	805-238-4722
❻ RANCHO MARIA	805-937-2019
❿ RIVER RIDGE	805-983-4653
❼ SANTA BARBARA	805-687-7087
⓫ SIMI HILLS	805-522-0803
❽ SOULE PARK	805-646-5633

REMINDER:
Except where noted, all courses are regulation size (6000+ yards), 18 hole, par 70-73 layouts with an average green fee of $24. Current maximum fee is noted next to course phone number.

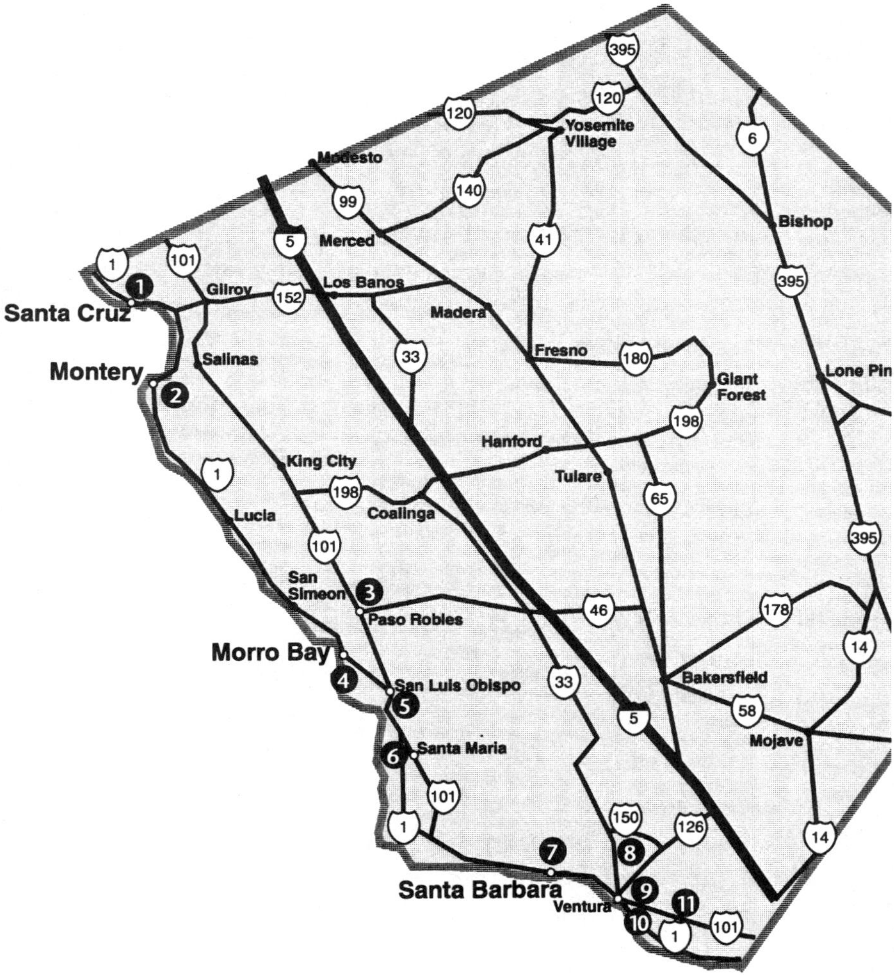
395
120
120
Yosemite Village
6
Modesto
140
99
5
Merced
41
Bishop
1
101
Gilroy
152
Los Banos
395
Santa Cruz
Madera
33
Fresno
180
Salinas
Montery
Lone Pin
Giant Forest
198
Hanford
1
King City
Tulare
198
65
Coalinga
Lucia
101
395
San Simeon
46
178
Paso Robles
14
Morro Bay
San Luis Obispo
33
Bakersfield
5
58
Mojave
Santa Maria
101
1
150
126
14
Santa Barbara
Ventura
1
101

DE LEVEAGA GOLF COURSE

401 Upper Park Rd.
Santa Cruz, CA 95065
408-423-7214 $32

A scenic stunner in the Santa Cruz mountains, set above Monterey Bay. One of the toughest course listed in this directory. Gorgeous, challenging layout—trees everywhere bordering rolling, sometimes hilly fairways. This course can eat you alive, but you'll love it nonetheless.

Directions: Off Hwy #1 take Morrisey exit to Fairmount turn right to Branciforte, turn right again and follow to course.

PACIFIC GROVE GOLF COURSE

77 Asilomar Blvd.
Pacific Grove, CA 93950
408-648-3175 $27

Surrounded by world famous $150+ courses and a natural beauty that is unsurpassed, this is a true diamond in the rough. Front nine meanders through the Del Monte forest without too much difficulty. But the back nine is what this course is all about. This seaside, Scottish-links layout set at the tip of the Monterey Peninsula provides a most spectacular and unobstructed view of the Pacific Ocean. Quite simply, affordable public golf at its best. *Note:* Beware the dreaded ice plant on the back nine.

Directions: From Hwy #1 in Monterey, take Hwy 68 west to Asilomar turn right to course.

PASO ROBLES GOLF AND CC
1600 Country Club Dr.
Paso Robles, CA 93446
805-238-4722 $22

A wonderful discovery just a few miles in from the coast. This one is a "sleeper." Comfortable, walkable course in a beautifully wooded setting. This pretty layout is not long but is very tight, with water coming into play on several holes. Great clubhouse facilities and staff. Relaxed atmosphere and a super value.

Directions: Paso Robles is located exactly halfway between San Francisco and Los Angeles. From Hwy 101 heading north take Spring St. exit to Niblick Bridge. Turn right and proceed to Country Club Dr. Turn right and follow to course. From Hwy 101 heading south take Spring St. exit and continue on Spring approximately 30 blocks to Niblick Bridge. Turn left and head east to Country Club Drive. Turn right and follow to course.

MORRO BAY GOLF COURSE
State Park Rd.
Morro Bay, CA 93442
805-772-4341 $26

A grand old seaside resort-type golf course, located inside Morro Bay State Park. Another example of the great golf available in this Central Coast region. Mature, challenging layout with lots of trees and ocean views on almost every hole. Just wonderful.

Directions: Exit Hwy #1 in Morro Bay and follow signs to "Morro Bay State Park".

AVILA BEACH RESORT

Avila Beach Rd.
Avila Beach, CA 93424
805-595-2307 $31

Located on the coast just south of San Luis Obispo, this is a marvelous resort course. Mid-length layout is tight with elevation changes, doglegs and the San Luis Creek coming into play on several holes. A good test in a great setting—super value.

Directions: From Hwy 1 south of San Luis Obispo take the Avila Beach exit and head west a couple of miles to the course on your right. Course is located at the San Luis Bay Inn.

RANCHO MARIA GOLF COURSE

1950 Casmalia Rd.
Santa Maria, CA 93455
805-937-2019 $25

You're out in the country here. Traditional, rolling layout with moderate difficulty in a very nice setting. A comfortable, pleasant golf experience.

Directions: Off Hwy 101 in Santa Maria take Clark Ave. exit drive west to Hwy 1 (2-3 miles) turn right. 1 mile to course.

SANTA BARBARA COMMUNITY GC

3500 McCaw Ave.
Santa Barbara, CA 93105
805-687-7087 $22

This hilly "locals" course offers some great views of the Channel Islands and the Pacific Ocean beyond. Traditional layout with length, set in the foothills above Santa Barbara. Pleasant and inexpensive round in this toney, scenic coastal resort town.

Directions: Off Hwy 101 in Santa Barbara, take Las Positas Rd. Drive east less than a mile to McCaw Ave. and turn left to course.

SOULE PARK GOLF COURSE

1033 East Ojai Ave.
Ojai, CA 93023
805-646-5633 $24

EAGLE AWARD

This place is spectacular. Set east of Santa Barbara in the mystical, magical Ojai Valley, adjacent to the Ojai Valley Inn, this course could sell memberships without changing a thing. Rolling traditional layout is in very good condition, and the clubhouse is one of the best in the state. First-rate facility in a magnificent setting. A California "must play."

Directions: From I-5 near Valencia take Hwy 126 west to Hwy 150 to Ojai and the course. From Hwy 101 in Ventura take Hwy 33 to Ojai and course. From Santa Barbara take 101 south to Hwy 150. East on 150 to Ojai and the course.

ELKINS RANCH GOLF COURSE

1386 Chambersburg Rd.
Fillmore, CA 93016
805-524-1440 $27

A great escape in a peaceful, rural setting. Tough test out in the country with trees and water everywhere. Beautiful course in good shape and very walkable.

Directions: From 101 or I-5 take Hwy 126 to Hwy 23. Go south to course.

RIVER RIDGE GOLF CLUB

2401 West Vineyard Ave.
Oxnard, CA 93030
805-983-4653 $24

This is a very difficult, links-style course, with water coming into play throughout including an island green on 14. Bring your "A" game to this well designed layout. Top-notch clubhouse adds to the experience.

Directions: Take Hwy 101 to Vineyard exit. Go west to course.

SIMI HILLS GOLF COURSE

5031 Alamo St.
Simi Valley, CA 93063
805-522-0803 $24

Excellent suburban golf. This well-designed course is a Ted Robinson creation and one of the better tracks in Southern Cal. Rolling, sometimes hilly layout is heavily treed with water coming into play on several holes. Tough course in good condition. Worth a trip.

Directions: Take Hwy 118 to Stearns St. exit. Turn right to Alamo and left to course.

CHAPTER TWO, PART 3

Los Angeles County

LA is everything you've heard it is—good and bad. The traffic and smog, the crazies, the beaches and above all, that year-round sunshine and near-tropical climate. But what you might not have heard is that it also has the best affordable public golf of any large metropolitan area in the world. Courses offering stunning settings, marvelous traditional architecture and championship layouts range in location from the cliffs of the Pacific Ocean to the base of the San Gabriel mountains. A marvelous mix of quality golf under $35.

Los Angeles County Quick Check

6	BROOKSIDE	818-796-0177
5	DE BELL	18-845-5052
11	EL DORADO	310-430-5411
3	GRIFFITH PARK	213-664-2255
2	KNOLLWOOD	818-363-8161
1	LOS ROBLES	805-496-6171
4	LOS VERDES	310-377-0338
9	MARSHALL CANYON	909-593-8211
10	MOUNTAIN MEADOWS	909-623-3704
3	RANCHO PARK	310-839-4374
11	RECREATION PARK	310-494-5000
8	SAN DIMAS CANYON	909-599-2313
7	SANTA ANITA	818-447-2331

REMINDER:
Except where noted, all courses are regulation size (6000+ yards), 18 hole, par 70-73 layouts with an average green fee of $24. Current maximum fee is noted next to course phone number.

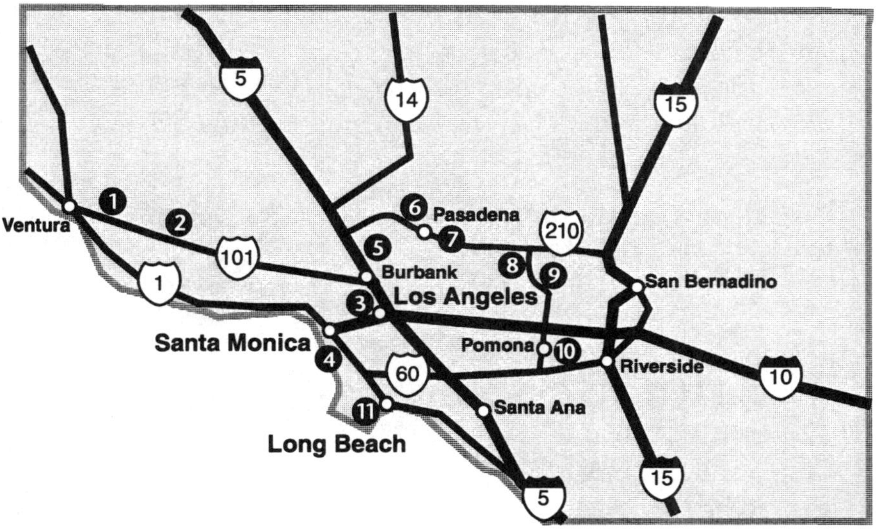
5
14
15
Ventura
1
2
101
1
6
Pasadena
7
210
5
Burbank
8
9
San Bernadino
3
Los Angeles
Santa Monica
Pomona
10
4
Riverside
10
60
11
Santa Ana
Long Beach
15
5

LOS ROBLES GOLF COURSE

299 S. Moorpark Rd.
Thousand Oaks, CA 91361
805-496-6171 $21

We start in the northern part of the county with a superb course and a personal favorite. Oak trees dominate this scenic, shorter layout that is in excellent condition. "Old country club" feel in a great setting. Super value—wonderful golf.

Directions: Take Hwy 101 to Moorpark Rd. Go west one block and turn right to course.

KNOLLWOOD GOLF COURSE

12040 Balboa Blvd.
Granada Hills, CA 91344
818-363-8161 $24

Highly rated suburban golf in San Fernando Valley. This hilly William Bell-designed "sleeper" has done nothing but improve over time. Great course, great setting and a great bargain.

Directions: Take Hwy 118 to Balboa Blvd. exit. Go north to course

RANCHO PARK GOLF COURSE

10460 West Pico Blvd.
Los Angeles, CA 90064
310-839-4374 $23

EAGLE AWARD

This is a very special place. A marvelous display of urban golf at its best. Surrounded by high rises, Rodeo Dr., Wilshire Blvd., etc, this rolling mature jewel sits in Rancho Park oblivious to all the "progress" around it. This championship layout has hosted PGA and Senior PGA events for years. A grand old "must play" in LA.

Directions: From I-405 in LA take Santa Monica Blvd exit east to Sepulvada Blvd. turn right to Pico and left to course. From I-10 in LA take Overland exit north to Pico and turn right to course.

GRIFFITH PARK

4730 Crystal Springs Dr.
Los Angeles, CA 90027
213-664-2255 $21

Located inside famous Griffith Park, this 36-hole complex is near many of LA's attractions in miles, but its picturesque, rural-like location offers a nice escape without traveling too far from the downtown area. Harding is the shorter of the two, while the Wilson course is higher rated. Both are mature, traditional layouts in a wonderful park setting.

Directions: From 101 or I-5 take Los Feliz Blvd. to Riverside Dr. into the park and follow to the courses.

LOS VERDES GOLF COURSE

7000 West Los Verdes Dr.
Rancho Palos Verdes, CA 90274
310-377-0338 $21

LA's answer to Torrey Pines. One of our most exciting "finds" just south of LAX and Redondo Beach. Sitting atop the cliffs at the edge of the Palos Verdes Peninsula, this course gives you some of the finest ocean views in the LA area. Country-club feel—plenty of challenge. On a clear day you can see Catalina Island. Super value under $30.

Directions: On Pacific Coast Hwy (Hwy 1) South of Redondo Beach take Hawthorne Blvd. west to Los Verdes Dr. and follow to course.

DE BELL GOLF COURSE

1500 Walnut Ave.
Burbank, CA 91504
818-845-5052 $20

Short, tight beautiful mountain side layout will keep you on your toes. Outstanding views of LA and San Fernando Valley. Fun course in a very attractive setting.

Directions: From I-5 take Olive Ave. east to Walnut. Turn right to course.

BROOKSIDE GOLF COURSE

133 Rosemont
Pasadena, CA 91103
818-796-0177 $30

36 holes in a park setting right at the Rose Bowl. The "Nay" course is the shorter of the two with some difficulty. The "Koiner" has been rated in the Top 10 of public courses in Southern California. Call first on weekends during football season.

Directions: Take I-210 to Seco/Mountain exit. Go south on Seco to Rosemont and follow to course.

SANTA ANITA GOLF COURSE

405 S. Santa Anita Ave.
Arcadia, CA 91006
818-447-2331 $22

This is a mature, pleasant course close to Santa Anita Race Track. Recently renovated and well maintained. Great design, challenging throughout and a super value.

Directions: Take I-210 to Santa Anita Ave. and travel south to course.

SAN DIMAS CANYON GOLF COURSE

100 Terrebone Ave.
San Dimas, CA 91773
909-599-2313 $27

Like Marshall Canyon, this course hugs the San Gabriels, offering a magnificent setting. Tremendous challenge, great layout and just a wonderful golf experience.

Directions: East on I-210 to San Dimas Ave. exit. Head north to Foothill Blvd. and turn right. Continue on Foothill to San Dimas Canyon Rd. Turn left and follow signs to course.

MARSHALL CANYON GOLF COURSE

6100 N. Stephens Ranch Rd.
La Verne, CA 91750
909-593-8211 $24

Dramatic setting at the base of the San Gabriel Mountains. This is a great find a little way out of town, but well worth it. Views everywhere. Very difficult greens require your full attention.

Directions: Take I-210 to Foothill Blvd. and continue on Foothill to Wheeler. Turn left (north) to Golden Hills and turn right. Continue to Stephens Ranch Rd. Turn left and follow to course.

MOUNTAIN MEADOWS GC

1875 N. Fairplex Dr.
Pomona, CA 91768
909-623-3704 $24

This is an exceptional golf course. A well-designed true test in excellent condition. Somewhat hilly with tree-lined fairways in a marvelous setting. All you could ask for in public golf under $30. One of the best in LA.

Directions: About 20 miles east of downtown LA on I-10. Take Fairplex Dr. exit and head north to course.

RECREATION PARK MUNICIPAL

5000 Deukmejian Dr.
Long Beach, CA 90804
310-494-5000 $22

Definitely your best bet in the Long Beach area. This former country club offers variety from hole to hole and is in excellent condition. It's a beautiful, mature, very walkable course. Top notch track.

Directions: Heading north on Hwy 1 turn left on 7th St. and follow to course. Heading south on Hwy 1 turn right on 7th and follow to course.

EL DORADO PARK GC

2400 Studebaker Rd.
Long Beach, CA 90815
310-430-5411 $22

Another example of solid golf in this area. Tree-lined fairways and small greens demand accuracy throughout this well-designed scenic course. Very comfortable.

Directions: Take I-405 to Studebaker Rd. exit and turn north to course.

CHAPTER TWO, PART 4

Orange, Riverside and San Bernardino Counties

This area is comprised of some of the biggest counties in the country and stretches from Disneyland to the desert. Many of its courses were built when this area was considered rural. You will find a variety of Southern California settings on these tracks, which for the most part are mature, traditional layouts in good condition. Because of the climate and condition, most of these courses offer golfers an exceptional value.

Orange, Riverside & San Bernardino Counties Quick Check

1	ANAHEIM HILLS	714-748-8900
1	DAD MILLER	714-991-5530
6	EL RIVINO	909-684-8905
5	GREEN RIVER	909-737-7393
8	HESPERIA	619-244-9301
6	INDIAN HILLS	909-360-2090
6	JURUPA HILLS	909-685-7214
7	LOS SERRANOS	909-597-1769
3	MEADOWLARK	714-846-1364
2	MILE SQUARE	714-545-7106
4	SAN CLEMENTE	714-361-8384

REMINDER:
Except where noted, all courses are regulation size (6000+ yards), 18 hole, par 70-73 layouts with an average green fee of $24. Current maximum fee is noted next to course phone number.

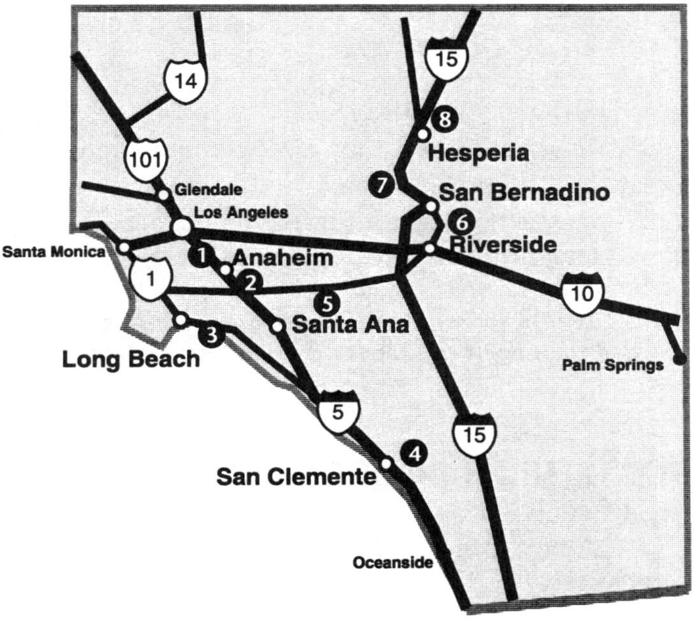
14
15
8
Hesperia
101
7
San Bernadino
Glendale
Los Angeles
6
Riverside
Santa Monica
1
Anaheim
1
2
10
5
Santa Ana
3
Long Beach
Palm Springs
5
15
4
San Clemente
Oceanside

"DAD" MILLER GOLF COURSE

430 N. Gilbert St.
Anaheim, CA 92804
714-991-5530 $22

There's something about this place. It's not long or particularly tough and not a course you'd drive a long way to play. But, it just feels good. Not far from Disneyland, maybe it's Mickey's influence. Great clubhouse, pleasant setting.

Directions: Take I-5 to Brookhurst St. exit go south to Crescent and turn right to Gilbert then left on Gilbert to course.

ANAHEIM HILLS GOLF COURSE

6501 Nohl Ranch Rd.
Anaheim, CA 92807
714-748-8900 $22

The key word here is hills. Lots of them— and steep. Don't try to walk this tough course. Set in an upscale residential area with a "club" feel, this course offers a wide variety of holes along with blind shots, water, trees and valleys. Keep it straight here.

Directions: From 91 Fwy exit at Imperial. Go right on Imperial and proceed three stop lights to Knoll Ranch Rd. Go left on Knoll Ranch Rd. 2 miles, course is on the left.

MILE SQUARE GOLF COURSE

10401 Warner Ave.
Fountain Valley, CA 92706
714-545-7106 $22

This is a well-maintained, mature public course. Wide-open walkers course with trees and water throughout. Afternoon winds can present some added difficulty. Very enjoyable golf for less than $30.

Directions: From I-405 take Brookhurst St. off ramp north to Warner Ave. Turn right to Ward St. and left to course.

MEADOWLARK GOLF COURSE

16782 Graham St.
Huntington Beach, CA 92649
714-846-1364 $25

Popular older course near the ocean. This traditionally Southern California layout features small greens, tree-lined fairways and water hazards on several holes. Good challenge in a pleasant setting at a great price.

Directions: From I-405 take Beach Blvd. exit and head west to Warner Ave. Turn right and continue for 2 miles to Graham. Turn right and follow to course.

SAN CLEMENTE GOLF COURSE

150 E. Avenida Magdalena
San Clemente, CA 92672
714-361-8384 $24

A wonderful William Bell course in this seaside resort town, featuring great ocean views on several holes. Easily walkable, open layout with some very difficult finishing holes. An extremely enjoyable round.

Directions: From I-5 heading south take Calafia make three right turns back over the freeway to Magdalena. Turn left and follow to course. From I-5 heading north take Avenida Magdalena exit to El Camino. Turn right and proceed one block to Magdalena. Turn left and follow to course.

GREEN RIVER GOLF CLUB

5215 Green River Rd.
Corona, CA 91720
909-737-7393
714-970-8411 $25

This older facility features two well-designed, rolling layouts set in a valley with the Santa Ana River running through both courses. Wind can be a factor. Trees everywhere. Orange course is longer and probably more difficult then the Riverside, but both play tight and feature small greens.

Directions: From Hwy 91 take the Green River Rd. exit. Head north to course (1 mile).

JURUPA HILLS COUNTRY CLUB

6161 Moraga Ave.
Riverside, CA 92509
909-685-7214 $24

This is a comfortable, suburban, "feel good" place and one of three fine courses in Riverside. A solid "locals" course that is easily walkable, heavily treed and features some of the fastest greens in all of California. Fun place, good value.

Directions: From Hwy 60 in Riverside take Van Buren/Etiwanda exit and head south on Van Buren for about 4 miles to Limonite Ave. Turn left and continue to Camino Real. Turn right to Linares and follow to course.

INDIAN HILLS COUNTRY CLUB

5700 Clubhouse Dr.
Riverside, CA 92509
909-360-2090 $28

Very hilly and tight with small greens. Not much room for error here. Scenic setting provides some great views, particularly on the back nine. Take a cart, it's included in the green fees.

Directions: From Hwy 60 in Riverside take Van Buren/Etiwanda exit Head south on Van Buren for about 4 miles to Limonite and turn left. Follow to Clay and turn left. Then make an immediate right on Lakeside Dr. and follow to course.

EL RIVINO COUNTRY CLUB

5530 El Rivino Rd.
Riverside, CA 92509
909-684-8905 $29

This beautifully maintained, rolling, rural course with its trees and lakes is reminiscent of Southern California from another era. Solid design provides a nice variety of holes in a comfortable setting just outside of town. Best bet in this area.

Directions: Take I-10 to Cedar Ave. exit and head south 3 miles to El Rivino Rd. Turn left and follow to course.

LOS SERRANOS COUNTRY CLUB

15656 Yorba Ave.
Chino Hills, CA 91709
909-597-1769 $30

Extremely enjoyable 36-hole facility in a beautiful Southern California setting. The par 74 South course is the more difficult of the two courses. It is a long, tough layout with six par 5s. Traditional, hilly and one of the top challenges in the area. The North is shorter and more easily walkable. Though not as trying as the South, it is not an easy course. Tighter layout and smaller greens place an emphasis on accuracy. Brand new, top-notch clubhouse is marvelous. All around good value here.

Directions: From Hwy 91 in Corona take Hwy 71 north to Chino Hills and the course. From I-10 or Hwy 60 near Pomona take Hwy 71 south to course.

HESPERIA GOLF AND CC

17970 Bangor Ave.
Hesperia, CA 92345
619-244-9301 $20

A scenic championship course in the high desert of remote Victor Valley north of San Bernardino. Testy, traditional, tree-lined, heavily bunkered layout. A very walkable and comfortable course in excellent condition. Relaxed, informal clubhouse and just outstanding public golf under $30.

Directions: From I-15 take Hesperia turnoff and head east on Main St. approximately 5 miles to I St. Turn right and continue for a little over a mile to Bangor. Turn left and follow to course.

CHAPTER TWO, PART 5

San Diego County

The local Chamber of Commerce claims it to be America's Finest City and believe me they're not that far off. Laid-back, friendly atmosphere with affordable accomodations for the traveler, wonderful beaches and great golf throughout the county. All this and an ideal year-round climate. Although no longer a sleepy, little Navy town, San Diego has retained that feel of what California used to be.

Note: Special mention should be made of Torrey Pines, one of the true jewels of golf. While it does not meet the price criteria we have set, it still represents a tremendous bargain. There are not many courses you can play that the pros also play, and we recommend you play Torrey Pines if you have the opportunity. We have included their 800# in our quick check.

San Diego County Quick Check

❶	BALBOA	619-235-1184
❶	BONITA	619-267-1103
❸	CASTLE CREEK	619-749-2422
❶	CORONADO	619-435-3121
❹	FALLBROOK	619-728-8334
❶	MISSION TRAILS	619-460-5400
❺	TORREY PINES	800-985-4653
❷	SINGING HILLS	619-442-3452

REMINDER:
Except where noted, all courses are regulation size (6000+ yards), 18 hole, par 70-73 layouts with an average green fee of $24. Current maximum fee is noted next to course phone number.

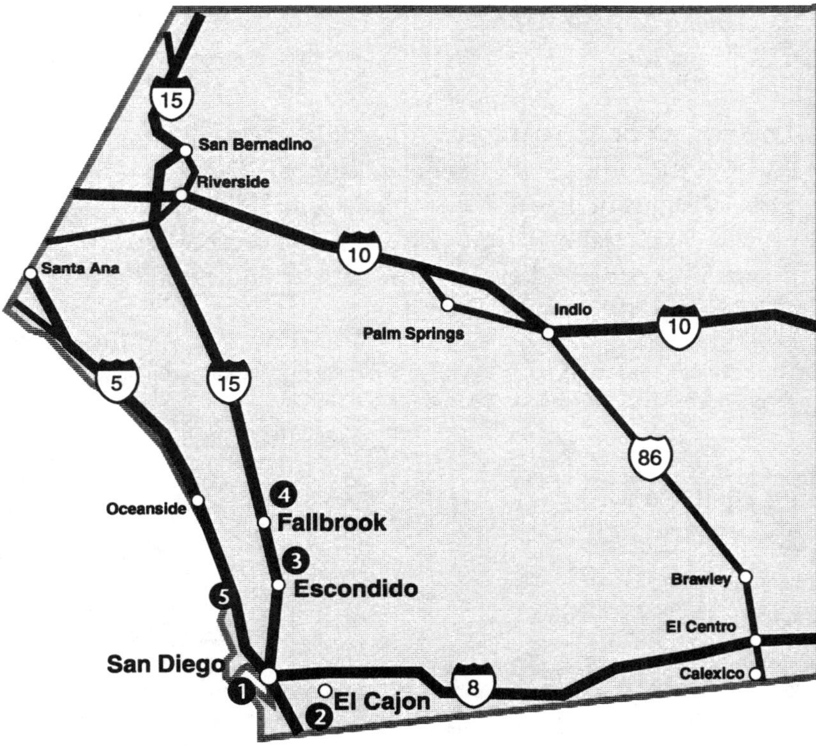
15
San Bernadino
Riverside
10
Santa Ana
Indio
10
Palm Springs
5
15
86
4
Oceanside
Fallbrook
3
Escondido
Brawley
5
El Centro
San Diego
Calexico
1
8
El Cajon
2

BALBOA PARK GOLF CLUB

2600 Golf Course Dr.
San Diego, CA 92102
619-235-1184 $31

This is your best bet for in-town golf in San Diego. Located in Balboa Park (home of the San Diego Zoo). This William Bell course, established in 1921, has been recently renovated and is in marvelous condition. Beautiful setting and great views. Traditional urban golf at its best.

Directions: Take I-5 to Pershing exit and go east to 26th. Turn right and follow to course.

CORONADO GOLF COURSE

2000 Visalia Row
Coronado, CA 92118
619-435-3121 $20

Great scenic location on San Diego Bay, providing views of the city, the harbor and the Hotel Del Coronado. Challenging, well maintained extremely enjoyable layout. A personal favorite, and at $20 the best deal in San Diego County.

Directions: Take I-5 to Coronado. After crossing bridge take first left possible then immediate left to Glorietta and turn right to course.

MISSION TRAILS GOLF COURSE

7380 Golfcrest Place
San Diego, CA 92119
619-460-5400 $29

Very pleasant, in-town, "locals" course near San Diego State. Tight, scenic valley setting requires accuracy over distance. Nice clubhouse facilities and an overall comfortable feel. Enjoyable golf with enough challenge to keep you on your toes.

Directions: Take I-8 east to College Ave. and go left one mile to Navajo St. turn right and continue on Navajo to Golfcrest Dr. and turn right to Golfcrest Place. Turn left into the course.

SINGING HILLS COUNTRY CLUB AND LODGE

3007 DeHasa Rd.
El Cajon, CA 92021
619-442-3425 $32

You'll love everything about this place. Ranked as one of the Top 100 public golf resorts in the country. One of the best "Under $35" golf experiences in California. Spectacular valley setting with tree-lined fairways and water coming into play on many holes. Highly challenging at all levels, this 36-hole complex is a "must play" if you're in the San Diego area.

Directions: Take I-8 to 2nd St. exit in El Cajon and go right. Continue five signals to Washington and turn left. This eventually becomes DeHasa. Continue on to course

BONITA GOLF CLUB

5540 Sweetwater Rd.
Bonita, CA 91902
619-267-1103 $20

Not far from downtown San Diego, this recently renovated course is located in a scenic valley setting surrounded by mountains. Not long, but the river and creeks that run through the course can present some difficulty. Great walking course in a pleasant, rural atmosphere, and at $20 a super bargain.

Directions: Take I-5 or I-405 south of San Diego to Hwy 54. Go east 4-5 miles to Sweetwater. Turn right and follow to course.

CASTLE CREEK COUNTRY CLUB

8797 Circle R Dr.
Escondido, CA 92026
619-749-2422 $32

Country club setting out in Escondido. This one's a "sleeper." Not long, but fun to play. Rural, woodsy layout recently upgraded. First-class clubhouse. Well worth the drive.

Directions: Take I-15 to Old Castle Rd. (east) turn left and follow signs to club.

FALLBROOK GOLF AND COUNTRY CLUB

2757 Gird Rd.
Fallbrook, CA 92028
619-728-8334 $27

Beautiful setting out in the country near Pala Mesa Resort. Tight, tree-lined, fun course requires some real shot making. Pleasant atmosphere, great value and easily walkable.

Directions: Take I-15 to Hwy 76 west to Gird Rd. then north approximately 2 miles to course.

CHAPTER 3

Hawaii

Hawaii and golf were made for each other. Ultimate year-round weather, slower pace of living and spectacular island settings combine to give you an ideal golf environment. If you can't enjoy golf here, try tennis. This is a place where you welcome "slow play" because it gives you more time to take in the beauty around you. In the last decade or so the state has undergone a "Golden Age" in golf construction, producing some of the finest resort facilities in the world.

As in Arizona, this international recognition brings with it "international pricing," putting them out of reach of this directory. However, what is available is wonderful. We have selected 10 courses that we feel represent the best value available on each island. Most are above-average facilities in magnificent settings. All will provide you an opportunity to be with some of the nicest people you will ever meet—the golfing residents of our 50th state.

Note: If the urge to splurge is out of control and you feel you must play one of those high-end resort courses, we recommend the following: On Kauai, either the Prince course at Princeville Resort or the Kiele course at Kauai Lagoons. On Maui, either the Plantation course at Kapalua or the Makena Golf Resort, and on the big island of Hawaii, it's Mauna Kea. All of these are "must play once in a lifetime" courses.

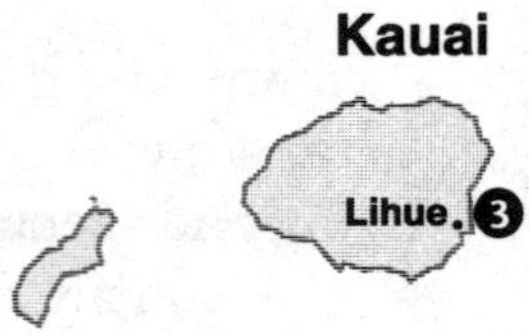

Hawaii Quick Check

2	ALA WAI-Oahu	808-296-4653
6	CAVANDISH-Lanai	No phone
5	HILO-Hawaii	808-959-7711
7	IRONWOOD HILLS-Molokai	808-567-6000
3	KUKUIOLONO-Kauai	808-332-9151
2	MOANALUA-Oahu	808-839-2411
1	PALI-Oahu	808-296-7254
4	WAIEHU-Maui	808-244-5934
3	WAILUA-Kauai	808-245-8092
2	WEST LOCH-Oahu	808-676-2210

REMINDER:
Except where noted, all courses are regulation size (6000+ yards), 18 hole, par 70-73 layouts with an average green fee of $24. Current maximum fee is noted next to course phone number.

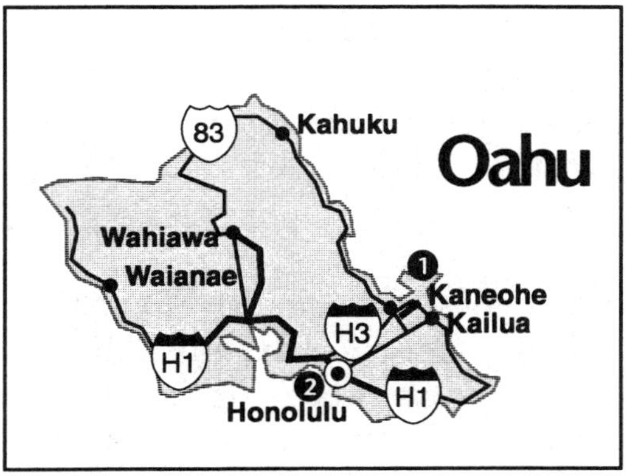
Oahu
83
Kahuku
Wahiawa
Waianae
1
Kaneohe
Kailua
H3
H1
2
Honolulu
H1

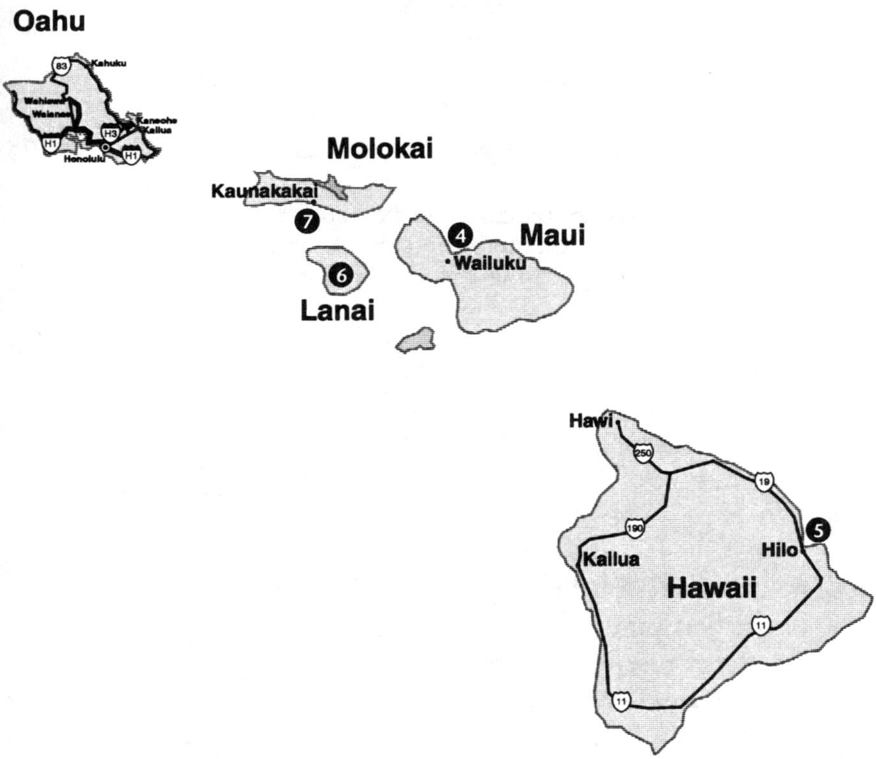
Oahu
Molokai
Kaunakakai
7
4
Maui
Wailuku
6
Lanai
Hawi
250
19
190
5
Hilo
Kailua
Hawaii
11
11

— OAHU —

PALI GOLF COURSE

45-050 Kamehameha Hwy
Kaneohe, HI 96744
808-296-7254 $24

With the spectacular cliffs of the Koolau Mountains on one side and the Pacific Ocean on the other, this peaceful, remote setting can be overwhelming. Less than 10 miles from Honolulu, yet far removed from even a hint of urban life. The layout itself is traditional in design, long and hilly, with very few level lies should you stray. Winds can add to the challenge making this a tough place to score. A tremendous value and a personal favorite on this island. Your best bet on Oahu.

Directions: From Honolulu take the Pali Hwy towards Kanehohe. After going through the tunnels continue on to Kamehameha Hwy. Turn left to the course.

WEST LOCH GOLF COURSE

91-1126 Olepekeupe Loop
Ewa Beach, HI 96706
808-676-2210 $24

Opened in 1990, this first-rate facility is the newest and one of the best public tracks on Oahu. Near Pearl Harbor, the course is still maturing and reaching its full potential. A mid-length layout with water hazards and lakes everywhere. Combine water and wind and you have a true test for golfers of all levels. Great clubhouse operation. Marvelous views of Honolulu and the Waianae Mountains. A very nice place to be.

Directions: Take the H-1 freeway to Ewa Beach. Exit at Hwy 76 and continue towards the ocean to West Loch Estates and turn left. Take immediate right to course.

ALA WAI MUNICIPAL GC

404 Kapahulu Ave.
Honolulu, HI 96815
808-296-4653 $24

Just a few blocks away from Waikiki Beach in the heart of Honolulu, with a great view of Diamond Head. Although not in the same class as Pali or West Loch, the location is what makes this place. You can't get much closer to the action and still be playing golf. Flat, easily walkable urban layout, with moderate difficulty. A fun outing that will not bruise your ego, your pocketbook or your handicap.

Directions: From Waikiki take Kalakaua towards Diamond Head to Kapahula Ave. Turn right to course.

MOANALUA GOLF COURSE

1250 Ala Aolani St.
Honolulu, HI 96819
808-839-2411 $18

Built in 1898, this is the birthplace of golf in Hawaii and one of the oldest courses west of the Mississippi. Very difficult full-size nine-holer that plays particularly tough the first time around. Narrow fairways, small greens and winds gusting through the valley create plenty of challenge. Scoring will improve second time around. Fun course with a bit of history and not far from Honolulu.

Directions: Take H-1 to Hwy 78. On Hwy 78 take Moanalua Valley exit and bear right. Continue on to course.

— KAUAI —

WAILUA MUNICIPAL GOLF COURSE

P.O. Box 1017
Kapaa, HI 96746
808-245-8092 $35

Kauai is the most beautiful island in the state. If it were a golf course, it would be rated 5-star; the "Augusta" of islands. So, it's only fitting that the best public course in the state is here. I first had the pleasure of playing this course in the 70s when I lived in the nearby town of Kapaa. I've been in love with it ever since. Located between two world-class golf resorts (Princeville and Kauai Lagoons) this wonderfully designed, oceanside layout is the work of local golf pro Toyo Shirai. This nationally recognized course represents the very best in "muni" golf. Well-maintained, demanding layout in a gorgeous setting highlighted by ocean and mountain vistas that are unforgettable. If you ever get the chance go to Kauai, play Wailua. You will remember both forever.

Directions: From Lihue take Hwy 56 to Kapaa. Course is on your right.

KUKUIOLONO GOLF COURSE

P.O. Box 1031
Kalaheo, HI 96741
808-332-9151 $10

Southwest of Wailua is another Toyo Shirai course. This one is a unique nine hole, par 36 located in heavily wooded Kukiolono Park. The elevated setting provides excellent views of the ocean and shoreline below. Remote, peaceful spot where you can play all day for $10. A tremendous bargain in Paradise.

Directions: From Lihue take Hwy 50 to Kalaheo. Turn left on Papaluna Rd. and follow to course.

— MAUI —

WAIEHU MUNICIPAL
P.O. Box 507
Wailuku, HI 96796
808-244-5934 $30

Not far from the airport in the town of Wailuku, this pretty seaside course is your best bet on Maui. Very walkable mid-length course with tree-lined fairways and tremendous Pacific Ocean views. Pleasant local experience and for the price, outstanding value. Just about everything else on the island is $100 or more.

Directions: From Kahului take Hwy 36 to Hwy 340 and take a right. Continue on to Waiehu Beach Rd. and take another right. Follow to course.

— HAWAII —

HILO MUNICIPAL GC
340 Haihai St.
Hilo, HI 96720
808-959-7711 $20

Off the beaten path in Hilo is a lovely tropical course offering great views of Hilo Bay and Mauna Kea. Pleasant mid-length layout is walkable and only moderately difficult. It rains a lot on this side of the island, but if you catch it on a sunny day, you're in heaven.

Directions: Take Hwy 11 towards Volcano and turn right at Puainako St. Take a left at Kinahole St. and a right on HaiHai St. and follow to course.

— LANAI —

CAVENDISH GOLF COURSE

P.O. Box 862
Lanai City, HI 96763 $5

Good, cheap golf in Paradise. Great views and a magnificent setting next to the Lodge at Koele. Tee it up and play as many holes as you like—green fees are $5 all day long!

Directions: Located adjacent to the Lodge at Koele in Lanai City.

— MOLOKAI —

IRONWOOD HILLS GOLF COURSE

Kalae Highway
Kualapuu, HI 96757
808-567-6000 $9

Basic golf at its best. Originally built by the Del Monte Corporation for its sugar workers, the course has been upgraded recently. Great fun in a great setting. Play all day on this remote island for under $10.

CHAPTER 4

Nevada

"Diamonds in the Rough" in the Silver State are as few and far between as a Royal Flush. Yes, there has been significant growth in new course construction recently, but these courses are high-end, $75-$150 facilities. However, we have uncovered 10 wonderful courses that will provide you with exceptional golf experiences in unique, high desert settings. Most of the courses are in the northern half of the state where the season runs from March to November with some Reno-Carson City courses staying open year round. Best bet? Mid-May to early October.

Golf in Southern Nevada is year-round but I would avoid the summer months due to excessive heat. Spring and fall are best. As far as good, affordable golf is concerned, Las Vegas is a desert with *no* oasis. There is a waystation in town (Las Vegas Golf Club) and an outpost near Hoover Dam in Boulder City, but that's about it. If you have the time and want to play some championship layouts, I would recommend the St. George area about 100 miles north of Las Vegas (*See Utah chapter for details*). Still, there are enough courses spread around the state to provide you with some different, dramatic challenges no matter where you land in this wide-open, friendly, 24 hour-a-day part of the West.

Nevada Quick Check

❷ Boulder City	702-293-9236
❹ Eagle Valley	702-887-2380
❻ Jackpot	702-755-2260
❶ Las Vegas GC	702-646-3003
❸ Rosewood Lakes	702-857-2892
❺ Ruby View	702-738-6212
❺ Spring Creek	702-753-6331
❼ Toana Vista	702-664-4300
❸ Washoe	702-828-6640

REMINDER:
Except where noted, all courses are regulation size (6000+ yards), 18 hole, par 70-73 layouts with an average green fee of $24. Current maximum fee is noted next to course phone number.

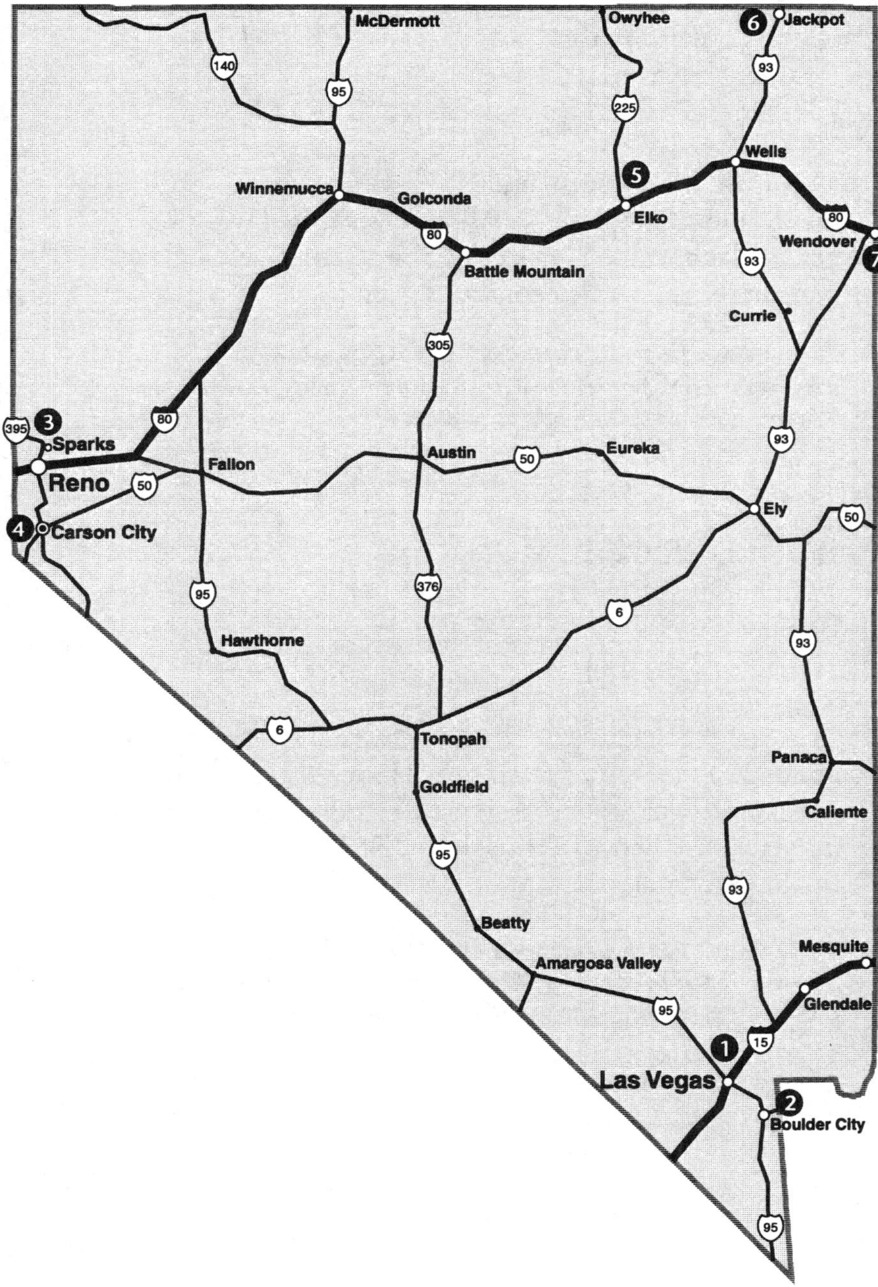
McDermott
Owyhee
6
Jackpot
140
95
93
225
Wells
5
Winnemucca
Golconda
Elko
80
80
Battle Mountain
Wendover
7
93
Currie
305
3
395
Sparks
80
Austin
50
Eureka
Reno
Fallon
50
93
Ely
50
4
Carson City
376
95
6
93
Hawthorne
6
Tonopah
Panaca
Goldfield
Caliente
95
93
Beatty
Mesquite
Amargosa Valley
Glendale
95
1
15
Las Vegas
2
Boulder City
95

LAS VEGAS GOLF CLUB

4300 W. Washington
Las Vegas, NV 89107
702-646-3003 $24

This is the only course under $75 in Las Vegas worth mentioning. Tree-lined, traditional, mature layout is very walkable and, considering the alternatives, a great bargain. Nice in-town course in good shape.

Directions: I-15 or Las Vegas Blvd. to Charleston and turn west to Valley View. Turn right on Valley View to Washington and turn left to course.

BOULDER CITY MUNICIPAL

1 Clubhouse Dr.
Boulder City, NV 89005
702-293-9236 $24

This is a pleasant, fairly flat, very walkable desert course about 20 miles out of town near Hoover Dam. Well maintained year-round. Fun user-friendly facility with moderate challenge, although the back nine can be difficult. Good value.

Directions: From Las Vegas take Hwy 93/95 towards Hoover Dam to Boulder City. Turn right at Buchannan Dr. (the only stop signal in town) and follow to course.

ROSEWOOD MUNICIPAL GOLF COURSE

6800 Pembroke Dr.
Reno, NV 89502
702-857-2892 $27

With Mt. Rose serving as its backdrop, this newer links layout in the high Sierra is a "must play" on your next trip to the Reno-Lake Tahoe area. Winding through environmentally sensitive wetlands, this walkable layout, though not very long, requires accuracy and thought. Lateral hazards on most holes. First-rate fairways (best in the state) reflect a commitment to maintenance that is commendable. Good staff and a good, solid course. Best bet in Reno.

Directions: Just outside of Reno on I-80 east towards Sparks take the Rock Blvd. exit. Turn right (south) on Rock and continue to course, approximately 4 miles. Rock Blvd. becomes Pembroke after you cross McCarron.

WASHOE COUNTY GOLF COURSE

2601 S. Arlington
Reno, NV 89509
702-828-6640 $22

Nice, old, traditional public track near downtown casinos. Back nine can present some real difficulty. Course condition has improved recently after a killer drought in the early '90s.

Directions; From I-80 or downtown take S.Virginia and head south to Plumb Ln. Turn right to Arlington and turn left to course.

EAGLE VALLEY GOLF COURSE

3999 Centennial Park Dr.
Carson City, NV 89706
702-887-2380 $33

This well-run 36-hole complex is a fine example of great public golf in Northern Nevada. The East course is a pleasant, enjoyable layout; wide open, well-maintained and walkable. The West course, however, is a completely different story. Don't let the dramatic setting distract you. This is target golf at its best. This championship links layout is one of the more challenging courses in the state, especially in the afternoon when the winds can come into play. Excellent alternative to the high-priced courses at Lake Tahoe.

Directions: Off Hwy 50 just east of Carson City on Centennial Park Drive.

RUBY VIEW GOLF COURSE

2100 Ruby View Dr.
Elko, NV 89801
702-738-6212 $22

One of the highest rated public courses in the Silver State, located in a booming, gold-mining outpost halfway between Reno and Salt Lake City. This is one of two excellent facilities in the Elko area. Just shy of 7000 yards from the tips, this well-designed, long course is wide, walkable and in excellent condition, featuring treelined fairways and heavily bunkered greens. A sleeper that will test you. Open from mid-March through October.

Directions: From I-80 take exit 303 (Red Lion) to Idaho St. and turn right. Follow to second stop sign and turn right again. Follow signs to course.

SPRING CREEK GOLF COURSE

451 E. Spring Creek Pkwy.
Elko, NV 89801
702-753-6331 $20

Narrow, short course in good condition with marvelous views of the scenic Ruby Mountains. Leave your driver in the bag. Accuracy is critical if you want to score here. Miss a fairway and you will become one with the cactus and sagebrush of the Nevada desert. Open mid-March through October.

Directions: From I-80 take exit 301 in Elko. Turn right at the stop light to 12th. Turn left and follow over bridge to next stop light (Memorial Highway). Turn left and on continue for approximately 10 miles to Spring Creek Parkway. Turn left and go 1 1/2 miles to Country Club and the course on your right.

JACKPOT GOLF CLUB

P.O. Box 388
Jackpot, NV 89825
702-755-2260 $20

A fine, rolling Robert Muir Graves design near the Nevada-Idaho border with large, very fast greens and doglegs coming into play on several holes. This is an enjoyable course in excellent condition, with wildlife roaming the grounds. Open mid-March through October.

Directions: From Hwy 93 in Jackpot signs will direct you to the course.

TOANA VISTA GOLF COURSE

2319 Pueblo Rd.
Wendover, NV 89883
702-664-4300 $24

This is desert golf. Located on the Nevada-Utah border next to the Bonneville Salt Flats where remote meets desolate. Tough, treeless course in very good condition. Well-designed layout with a good variety of holes featuring narrow fairways, lots of water and treacherous greens. A solid course. Open mid-March through October. *Note:* Excellent Nevada-style accommodations in town.

Directions: From I-80 take Wendover exit. Head west past the casinos and to the course.

CHAPTER 5

Oregon

Oregon has a fine tradition of excellent public golf. Its forests, mountains, waterways and high-desert provide some outstanding golf settings. The City of Portland has long been recognized as having some of the best urban golf facilities in the country. And now the Bend area is becoming a nationally recognized golf destination resort spot. Throughout the state you will find a good selection of challenging layouts in a relaxing and scenic atmosphere. Most courses are open year-round but as you know, it rains. It rains a lot, actually, mostly in the winter months. Your best bet? Late spring through early fall with July, August and September being ideal. In this chapter we start in southern Oregon along the I-5 corridor and work our way north to the Portland area then east through the Columbia Gorge and down to Bend.

Oregon Quick Check

❶	Cedar Links	541-773-4373
⓬	Crooked River Ranch	541-548-0278
❽	Eastmoreland	503-775-2900
❷	Emerald Valley	541-895-2174
❻	Forest Hills	503-357-3347
❽	Heron Lakes	503-289-1818
❾	Indian Creek	541-386-7770
❺	McNary	503-393-4653
⓭	Meadow Lakes	541-447-7113
❸	Ocean Dunes	541-997-3232
❼	Quail Valley	503-324-4444
❿	Resort at the Mtn	800-669-4653
⓮	Rivers Edge	541-389-2828
❽	Rose City	503-253-4744
❺	Salem	503-363-6652
❸	Sandpines	541-997-1940
❶	Stone Ridge	541-830-4653
⓫	Tokatee	541-822-3220
❹	Trysting Tree	541-752-3332

REMINDER:
Except where noted, all courses are regulation size (6000+ yards), 18 hole, par 70-73 layouts with an average green fee of $24. Current maximum fee is noted next to course phone number.

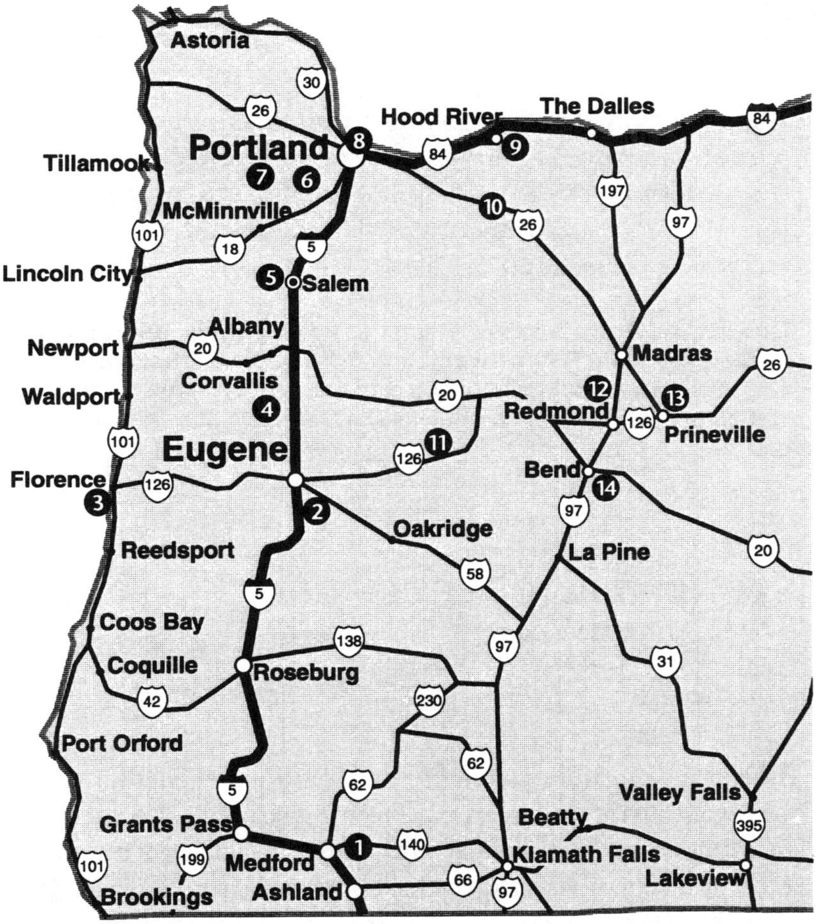
Astoria
Portland
Tillamook
McMinnville
Lincoln City
Salem
Albany
Newport
Corvallis
Waldport
Eugene
Florence
Reedsport
Coos Bay
Coquille
Roseburg
Port Orford
Grants Pass
Medford
Brookings
Ashland
Hood River
The Dalles
Madras
Redmond
Prineville
Bend
Oakridge
La Pine
Valley Falls
Beatty
Klamath Falls
Lakeview
1
2
3
4
5
6
7
8
9
10
11
12
13
14
30
26
84
197
97
101
18
5
20
126
58
138
42
230
62
31
395
140
199
66

CEDAR LINKS GOLF COURSE

3155 Cedar Links Dr.
Medford, OR 97501
541-773-4373 $20

Wide open fairways and rolling terrain make this a pleasant challenge. This was the only 18-hole course in the area for many years and remains a favorite of the locals. Watch out for the water. There's not a lot of it, but what's there can sneak up on you.

Directions: From I-5 take Crater Lake hwy (Exit 30) north to Delta Waters Rd. Turn right to Springbrook (there are two streets called Springbrook, take the second and turn right) and follow to Cedar Links Dr. Turn left and follow to course.

STONERIDGE GOLF CLUB

500 E, Antelope Road
Eagle Point, OR 97524
541-830-4653 $20

This is a beautiful new course on the fringe of Medford. Great attention has been paid to maintenance and to keeping the natural beauty of the area intact. Lots of old oaks and lots of water give this course a mature feeling. The excellent design will challenge you from start to finish. The country setting makes for a peaceful round and a pleasant day.

Directions From I-5 take exit 30 and go north on Hwy 62 approximately 6 miles to Hwy 140. Turn right, go 3 miles then right on East Antelope Rd.

EMERALD VALLEY GOLF CLUB

83293 Dale Kuni Rd.
Creswell, OR 97426
541-895-2174 $25

Challenging championship course in great condition with heavily bunkered, fast greens. Country club feel in a beautiful rural setting along the Willamette River. This is your best bet in the Eugene area.

Directions: Emerald Valley directions From I-5 take Creswell exit #182. Go east over the freeway 1 mile to Dale Kuni Rd. Turn left and follow to course.

OCEAN DUNES GOLF LINKS

3345 Munsel Lake Rd.
Florence, OR 97439
541-997-3232 $25

What this tough little course lacks in length it more than makes up in tightness. Some of the fairways are pencil thin, and all are surrounded by sand dunes that are heavy with tall dune grasses. If you tend to stray off the tee, bring a lot of balls. Afternoon winds add to flavor. This one is a challenge you'll want to take again after you get a feel for it. Lots of fun.

Directions: From Hwy 101 turn east on Munsel Lake Rd. and follow to course.

SANDPINES GOLF RESORT

1201 35th St.
Florence, OR 97439
541-997-1940
800-917-4653 $50

This is the finest public golf course in the state. Although there are days of the week and times of the year when it can be played under $35, the highest posted rate exceeds the limit set in this directory. But, like Torrey Pines in San Diego, we list it here because of its exceptional value. This Rees Jones design was voted the Top New Resort Course in the country when it opened in the early '90s. Spectacular layout reminiscent of Monterey Peninsula courses in California. An unforgettable golf experience.

Directions: Take Hwy 101 to 35th St. Head west and follow to course.

TRYSTING TREE GOLF CLUB

34028 Electric Rd.
Corvallis, OR 97333
541-752-3332 $23

A bit off the beaten path next to Oregon State University, you'll find one of the better courses in the state. Tough and long. Most of the difficulty in this links-style layout lies in the bunkering, heavy rough and very quick greens. Good course, great value.

Directions: Take I-5 to Hwy 34. Head west toward Corvallis approximately 9 miles to Electric Road. Turn right and follow to course.

McNARY GOLF CLUB

6255 River Rd. N.
Keizer, OR 97303
503-393-4653 $24

This semi-private course has a country club feel about it. Well-manicured with exceptional maintenance from the parking lot to the 18th green. Fairly open layout with lots of water and sand. The course has held up well over the years. For a real challenge, play from the blues.

Directions: From I-5 in Salem take exit 260 and head west approximately 1.5 miles to River Rd. and turn right. Immediately turn left on McNary Estates Rd. and follow to course.

SALEM GOLF CLUB

2025 Golf Course Rd. S.
Salem, OR 97302
503-363-6652 $28

Very stylish semi-private club. Not long, but narrow, tree-lined fairways demand accuracy. A beautiful older course in the Capitol City. Well-maintained and very walkable with a great clubhouse.

Directions: From I-5 heading south take exit 253 and go west on Mission to Commercial. Turn left and follow to Owens. Turn right and follow to course (approximately 2 miles). From I-5 heading North take exit 248 and go north on Commercial a ways to Owens. Turn left and follow to course.

FOREST HILLS GOLF CLUB

36250 SW Tongue Lane
Cornelius, OR 97113
503-357-3347 $22

This mature, scenic course is one of the prettiest in the state. Rolling, rural setting with enough challenge to keep your attention. Great views in an extremely pleasant atmosphere. Definitely worth a trip.

Directions: From Hwy 8 in Cornelius take Hwy 219 and head south to Tongue Lane. Turn right and follow to course.

QUAIL VALLEY GOLF COURSE

12565 NW Aerts Rd.
Banks, OR 97106
503-324-4444 $25

Newer, very non-Oregon links course out in Banks. This beautifully manicured, still maturing layout is an exciting place to play. Not long but certainly not easy. Wonderful place worth a look.

Directions: From Hwy 26 west of Hillsboro take Hwy 6 exit and follow to course on your right.

EASTMORELAND GOLF COURSE

2425 SE Bybee
Portland, OR 97202
503-775-2900 $20

If you can only play one round in Portland, this is where you want to play it. This great, traditional course has hosted the City Championship for more than 70 years and has been the site for the U.S. Public Links Championship. This well-designed course features narrow fairways with trees everywhere. Highly rated nationally and one of the top public courses in the Pacific Northwest.

Directions: Take 99E (McLaughlin) south to Eastmoreland/Reed College turnoff. Turn right on Bybee and follow to course.

HERON LAKES

3500 N. Victory Rd.
Portland, OR 97217
503-289-1818 $25

This facility features two 18-hole courses designed by Robert Trent Jones, Jr. and both are under $30—You gotta love it. The Great Blue is a nationally ranked championship layout requiring every shot in your bag. This rolling links-style course is one of the toughest in the state and a true diamond in the rough. Prepare to be tested. Although not as difficult as Great Blue, the Greenback Course is a very walkable, well-designed, traditional layout that is thoroughly enjoyable.

Directions: From I-5 take exit 306B (Portland International Raceway) and follow signs to course.

ROSE CITY GOLF COURSE

2200 NE 71st
Portland, OR 97213
503-253-4744 $20

Wonderful in-town golf. Traditional, mature course is heavily treed with water coming into play on the back nine. Somewhat hilly but walkable. Good course.

Directions: From I-84 take exit 4 to NE 74th and turn left to Tilamook St. Turn left again and follow to course

INDIAN CREEK GOLF COURSE

3605 Brookside Dr.
Hood River, OR 97031
541-386-7770 $29

The vistas are as nice as the course and both are gorgeous. There's some room to miss a shot or two here, but you'll find yourself with a number of hilly lies on or off the fairway. Solid design provides lots of challenge. Fall rounds can be especially beautiful. (*Note*: Another fine course in the Gorge area, and not far from here, is Skamania Lodge Golf Course in Stevenson, WA. See Washington chapter for complete listing.)

Directions Off I-84 take exit 62. This becomes Cascade. Take Cascade 1 mile to 13th. Go right on 13th 1 mile to Brookside Drive. Go right and follow 3/4 mile to course.

THE RESORT AT THE MOUNTAIN

68010 E. Fairway Ave.
Welches, OR 97067
1-800-669-4653 $33

If you're looking for an "Oregon Experience," this is the place. This full-service mountain resort, less than an hour from Portland, offers 27 holes of scenic valley golf within the Mt. Hood National Forest. Recently upgraded and expanded, this fine facility features three separate, well-maintained nines with excellent greens. Any combination will provide you with 18 holes of relaxing, "get away from it all" golf. Just a wonderful place.

Directions: Approximately 40 miles east of Portland off Hwy 26 in Welches.

TOKATEE GOLF CLUB

54947 McKenzie Hwy
Blue River, OR 97413
541-822-3220 $28

Here is a Ted Robinson jewel tucked back in the foothills of the Cascades. This well-designed, beautiful layout allows you to work up to your game on the front nine but tightens up considerably on the back. One of the highest rated courses in Oregon, with a great staff and efficient maintenance crew. A bit out of the way, but if you are anywhere near this gorgeous area, go for it!

Directions: From Eugene take Hwy 126 and head east about 47 miles (a picturesque ride along the McKenzie River). Course is on your left. Entrance is visible from Hwy 26.

CROOKED RIVER RANCH

5195 Club House Rd.
Crooked River Ranch, OR 97760
541-548-0278 $22

Hidden away, high-desert resort. Wide-open course beautifully maintained running through canyons along the Crooked River. Fantastic setting and a fun experience in the Bend-Redmond area.

Directions: Approximately 5 miles north of Redmond and on the north side of Terrebone off Hwy 97. Turn west at sign and follw signs to the course (approximately 7 miles).

MEADOW LAKES GOLF COURSE

300 Meadow Lakes Dr.
Prineville, OR 97754
541-447-7113 $25

EAGLE AWARD

This is an excellent example of all the things a new municipal course can be. A championship links-style course with water on *every* hole. First-rate club house facilities, a great driving range and an award winner for its environmental policies. Great golf, great service, great price. The epitome of a true diamond in the rough.

Directions: From Portland or Madras take Hwy 26; from Redmond take Hwy 126 east and from Bend take Hwy 97 north to 126 east on to Prineville and the course located right in town.

RIVERS EDGE GOLF CLUB

400 Pro Shop Dr.
Bend, OR 97701
541-389-2828 $29

This wonderful Robert Muir Graves resort course is your best bet in the Bend-Redmond area. A highly-rated, affordable course in a fairly expensive golf area. Somewhat hilly but walkable, this course provides challenge at all levels of play in stunning surroundings. Great clubhouse, good staff.

Directions: From Hwy 97 in Bend take Mt. Washington Dr. (The River House) and follow to course.

CHAPTER 6

Utah

Here you will find pure golf heaven. A bargain hunting golfer's dream come true. When I first started the research for this book more than three years ago, Utah was not part of the equation. But, the more I traveled the Western states, the more I kept hearing from other golfers about the courses in Utah. Their descriptions were so glowing and exciting that I knew a trip was in order. *What a place:* Spectacular scenery, high-level course maintenance, excellent walk-on access, magnificent settings, country club amenities and green fees in the mid-teens (mid-20s with cart.) Just unbelievable. Prepare to be stunned. The Utah Golf Association and everyone involved deserves congratulations for their commitment to quality, affordable golf for the public player.

We have divided the state into two sections: The North, which encompasses the Greater Salt Lake area from Provo to Logan, and the South, which consists mainly of courses in the St. George area. The Northern courses offer magnificent mountain settings with an abundance of trees and water, while the Southern courses present fine displays of desert golf.

Northern golf is seasonal, Mar.-Apr. thru Sept.-Oct. Southern golf is advertised as "year-round" but it can get pretty hot in July-Aug. and downright nippy in Dec.-Feb. Similar to weather in Las Vegas which is less than two hours south.

Anywhere you go in this state you will find challenging courses of all types in the midst of exquisite natural scenery.

Utah Quick Check

❻ Bonneville	801-583-9513
❺ Bountiful Ridge	801-298-6040
❹ Davis Park	801-544-0401
❻ Eaglewood	801-299-0088
⓫ Green Springs	801-673-7888
❾ Hobble Creek	801-489-6297
❽ Homestead	801-654-1102
❶ Logan River	801-750-0123
⓬ Moab	801-259-6488
❷ Mount Ogden	801-629-8700
❼ Park City	801-523-2135
⓫ St. George	801-634-5854
❿ Sky Mountain	801-635-7888
⓫ Southgate	801-628-0000
⓫ Sunbrook	801-634-5866
❹ Valley View	801-546-1630
❽ Wasatch Mountain	801-654-0532
❻ West Ridge	801-966-4653
❸ Wolf Creek	801-745-3365

REMINDER:
Except where noted, all courses are regulation size (6000+ yards), 18 hole, par 70-73 layouts with an average green fee of $24. Current maximum fee is noted next to course phone number.

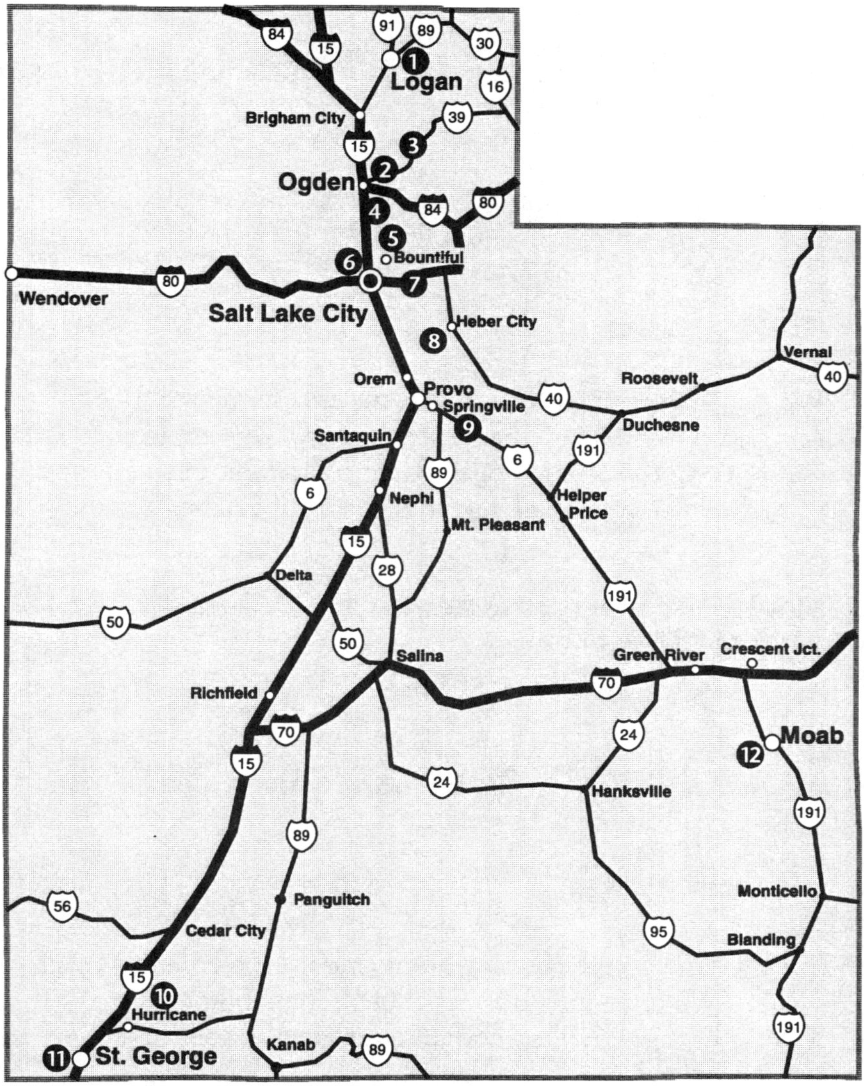
84
15
91
89
30
1
Logan
16
Brigham City
39
3
15
2
Ogden
4
84
80
5
Bountiful
6
80
7
Wendover
Salt Lake City
Heber City
8
Vernal
Roosevelt
40
Orem
Provo
40
Springville
9
Duchesne
Santaquin
6
191
89
6
Nephi
Helper
Price
Mt. Pleasant
15
28
Delta
191
50
50
Salina
Green River
Crescent Jct.
70
Richfield
70
24
Moab
12
15
24
Hanksville
191
89
Monticello
Panguitch
56
95
Cedar City
Blanding
15
10
Hurricane
191
Kanab
89
11
St. George

— THE NORTH —

Greater Salt Lake from Logan to Provo including Park City and Midway

LOGAN RIVER GOLF COURSE

550 W. 1000 South
Logan, UT 84321
801-750-0123 $15

We start this section with one of the nicest courses in northern Utah. As the name would imply this course winds along the scenic Logan River in and out of trees, providing extreme challenge in a beautiful Cache Valley setting.

Directions: Take Hwy 89 to Park Road (just out side of town) and follow to course.

MOUNT OGDEN GOLF COURSE

1787 Constitution Way
Ogden, UT 84403
801-629-8700 $15

Hilly, scenic course running along and up the base of Mt Ogden. We recommend a cart here. Challenging course with trees, tight doglegs and difficult greens. Your best bet in Ogden.

Directions: From Harrison Blvd (Hwy 203) just north of Weber State College turn east on 32nd St. to Taylor. Turn left and follow to course.

WOLF CREEK RESORT

3900 N. Wolf Creek Dr.
Eden, UT 84310
801-745-3365 $28

Championship resort layout about 15 miles from Ogden. Another excellent example of quality golf under $30 available in this state. Front and back nine completely different, but the stunning setting remains constant.

Directions: From Ogden take Hwy 39 east approximately 10 miles to Hwy 158. Turn left and follow to Eden and the course.

VALLEY VIEW

2501 E. Gentile
Layton, UT 84041
801-546-1630 $15

Has been rated in the Top 75 public courses in the country. Well-maintained with an excellent variety of holes and some tricky greens. This scenic mountain course represents "muni" golf at its best.

Directions: Take Hwy 89 in Layton to E. Gentile (1000 North) and follow to course.

DAVIS PARK GOLF COURSE

1074 E. Nicholls Rd.
Fruit Heights, Utah 84037
801-544-0401 $15

A very nice, mature local public track just north of Salt Lake. Not particularly long, beautifully maintained and easily walkable with enough challenge to make it interesting, especially on the greens.

Directions: Take Hwy 89 to Nicholls Rd. and follow to course.

BOUNTIFUL RIDGE GOLF COURSE

2430 South Bountiful Blvd.
Bountiful, UT 84010
801-298-6040 $15

EAGLE AWARD

And the hits just keep on coming. Another great mountain course with challenge and spectacular views of the Great Salt Lake. Thoroughly enjoyable golf at an outstanding facility.

Directions: Take I-15 north to Hwy 89 exit to Orchard (Texaco station) Turn right and take Eaglewood to the end. Turn left on Bountiful and follow to course.

EAGLEWOOD GOLF COURSE

1110 E. Eaglewood Dr.
North Salt Lake, UT 84054
801-299-0088 $17

Fantastic newer course that is still maturing. Could develop into one of the finest public golf facilities in the Salt Lake area. Country club atmosphere with high levels of maintenance, great design, panoramic views and a marvelous clubhouse that is home to the Utah Golf Assn. and the Utah Golf Hall of Fame.

Directions: Take I-15 north to Hwy 89 exit to Orchard (Texaco station). Turn right and take Eaglewood to course.

BONNEVILLE GOLF COURSE

954 Connor St.
Salt Lake City, UT 84108
801-583-9513 $17

Best urban golf course in the state. Wonderful, mature, well-maintained muni in a park setting at the base of the Wasatch Mountains. Long and rolling, with trees everywhere.

Directions: In Salt Lake take Foothill Blvd. (2100 East) to Sunnyside. Turn East and take the very first right (less than a block) and follow to course.

WEST RIDGE GOLF COURSE

5055 S. W. Ridge Blvd.
West Valley City, UT 84118
801-966-4653 $17

Great, new links-style course set on ridge in the west valley. Not long, but as with most links designs, accuracy is critical. Westside location provides unique panorama of the entire valley and the mountains.

Directions: Take 4700 South approximately 4 miles west of I-215 to West Ridge Blvd. Turn left and follow to course.

PARK CITY GOLF COURSE

P.O.Box 2067
Park City, UT 84060
801-523-2135 $25

Scenic mountain course located in the heart of this up-scale resort town. Well-maintained, first-class facility with streams and lakes coming into play throughout. Definitely worth the 30-mile drive from Salt Lake.

Directions: From Salt Lake take I-80 east to exit 145 and go right (south) on Hwy 224. Follow to course.

HOMESTEAD RESORT

700 N. Homestead Dr.
Midwy, UT 84049
801-654-1102 $30

This classy, full-service country resort offers a championship layout, winding through the beautiful Snake Creek Valley in a setting reminiscent of Switzerland. You won't want to leave.

Directions: Coming from the North take Hwy 40 to Heber City and go west to Midway and follow Homestead Resort signs to course. From South take Hwy 189 to Heber City and go west to Midway and follow to course.

WASATCH MOUNTAIN STATE PARK

Midway, UT 84049
801-654-0532 $18

Just up the road from Homestead is a marvelous public facility at the backside base of the Wasatch Mountains. Three "nines" to choose from: mountain, lake or valley. Any combination will be rewarding. Top-notch facility provides an exhilarating golf experience.

Directions: Same as above for Homestead. Course is on same road just little beyond the Resort.

HOBBLE CREEK GOLF COURSE

Hobble Creek Canyon Rd.
Springville, UT 84663
801-489-6297 $17

Sheer beauty hidden away from all of civilization. A true diamond in the rough! This magnificent, completely natural layout runs through heavily forested Hobble Creek Canyon, providing a serene and challenging experience. Just wonderful. One of the nicest golf outings you can ever imagine.

Directions: From I-15 take Springville exit 263 and head east 3 miles to 1300 East. Turn right and follow to course (approximately 4 miles).

— THE SOUTH —

Cedar City, St George/ Zion National Park area and Moab

SKY MOUNTAIN GOLF COURSE

1030 N. 2600 West
Hurricane, UT 84737
801-635-7888 $26

This new course in Hurricane, on the road to Zion, will take your breath away! With its canyons, mountains, river and red rock bluffs, this place is its own "mini" national park. One of the finest displays of southwestern desert golf I have ever seen, at any price. A "must play" in southern Utah.

Directions: From I-15 north of St. George take Hurricane (exit 16) and head west approximately 6 miles to 2600 West (Comfort Inn). Turn left and follow to course.

GREEN SPRINGS GOLF COURSE

588 N. Green Springs Dr.
Washington, UT 84720
801-673-7888 $27

This highly regarded layout has a country club feel. Another scenic beauty in the St. George area. Tough target golf in a magnificent desert setting with canyons separating many fairways and greens. A course you will long remember.

Directions: Off I-15 take Washington (Exit 10) and head west on Green Springs to course.

SUNBROOK GOLF COURSE

2240 W. Sunbrook Dr.
St George, UT 84770
801-634-5866 $29

This Ted Robinson layout is one of the highest rated, most challenging courses in the state. If you want to find out where your game really is, this championship course will let you know. A stunning golf course with great variety, several signature holes and spectacular vistas. A "must play" course.

Directions: From I-15 take Bluff St (Exit 6) west to Sunset Blvd. (Hwy 16). Turn left and continue to Dixie Dr. Turn left and follow to course.

SOUTHGATE GOLF COURSE

1975 S. Tonaquint Dr.
St George, UT 84720
801-628-0000 $25

Pleasant layout with an extremely difficult back nine that will definitely grab your attention. Good practice facilities and all-around maintenance shows what a city- owned course can achieve.

Directions: From I-15 take Bluff St. (Exit 6) west and make first left (Hilton Dr). Follow around to course.

ST. GEORGE GOLF CLUB

2190 S. 1400 East
St George, UT 84770
801-634-5854 $25

Recently renovated older course provides good test especially from the back tees. Well-maintained "muni" layout is very popular with the locals and tourists alike. Nice setting.

Directions: Off I-15 take Bloomington (Exit 4) and head east on Brigham Rd. to River Rd. Turn left and follow around to Ft. Pierce Dr. Turn left and then make first left to course.

MOAB GOLF COURSE

2705 S. E. Bench Rd.
Moab, UT 84532
801-259-6488 $18

Off the beaten path along the Colorado River, set at the entrance to Arches National Park. This one's a "sleeper." Not a particularly long course but plenty of challenge with a stunning Southwest setting.

Directions: Coming from the west on I-70 take exit 180 (Hwy 191). Head south to Moab and the course. From the east on I-70 take exit 202 (Hwy 128) and head south to Moab and the course.

CHAPTER SEVEN

Washington

Washington is a golf-rich area that offers an outstanding array of first-class, affordable courses. Throughout the state you will find marvelous courses with spectacular scenery, demanding layouts, wonderful clubhouse facilities and a serious commitment to course maintenance. The only drawback here is weather. Rain comes into play quite a bit. Most courses remain open year-round and "play it by ear." Some actually shut down for the winter season. Inclement weather doesn't seem to bother the golf-crazed locals here, but you would want to avoid the winter months and plan your excursions in the May to October time period, with late June through mid-September being ideal.

We've divided the state into two sections. The first being Western Washington, which runs the I-5 corridor from south to north branching out to include the Olympic Peninsula and the Hood Canal areas. The second section covers Central and Eastern Washington. We start in the Columbia Gorge, move east to the Tri-Cities area, then to a great run of courses along the eastern foothills of the Cascades, and finally, a golf mini-mecca in Spokane.

Washington Quick check

7	Alderbrook	360-898-2560
17	Alta Lake	509-923-2359
11	Avalon	360-757-1900
15	Canyon Lakes	509-582-3736
3	Capitol City	360-491-5111
18	Creek at Qualchan	509-448-9317
8	Dungeness	360-683-6344
6	Gold Mountain	360-674-2363
18	Hangman Valley	509-448-1212
13	Homestead	800-354-1196
5	Horseshoe Lake	206-857-3326
18	Indian Canyon	509-747-5353
16	Kahler Glen	509-763-4025
10	Kayak Point	360-652-9676
6	Lakeland Village	360-275-6100
17	Lake Chelan	509-682-5421
12	Lake Padden	360-738-7400
4	Lake Spanaway	206-531-3660
16	Leavenworth	509-548-7267
1	Lewis River	360-225-8254
5	Madrona Links	206-851-5465
19	Meadowood	509-255-9539
4	North Shore	360-927-1375
2	Riverside	360-748-8182
12	Shuksan	360-398-8888
14	Skamania Lodge	509-427-2541
12	Sudden Valley	360-734-6435
3	Tumwater Valley	360-943-9500
9	West Seattle	209-935-5187

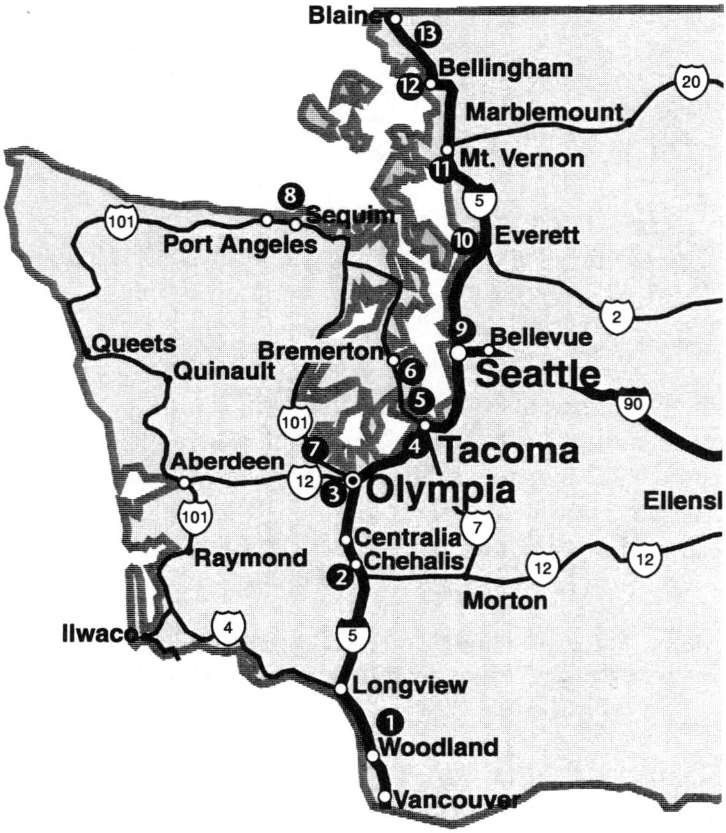

Blaine
13
Bellingham
12
20
Marblemount
Mt. Vernon
11
5
8
Sequim
101
Port Angeles
10
Everett
2
9
Bellevue
Queets
Bremerton
6
Seattle
Quinault
5
90
101
4
Tacoma
7
Aberdeen
12
3
Olympia
Ellensl
101
7
Centralia
Raymond
Chehalis
2
12
12
Morton
Ilwaco
4
5
Longview
1
Woodland
Vancouver

Blaine
Oroville
Laurier
Bellingham
97
Colville
20
Marblemount
Mt. Vernon
Omak
395
5
Twisp
2
Sequim
101
Port Angeles
Everett
Coulee Dam
17
18
155
19
2
Spokane
Queets
Bellevue
16
Bremerton
Quinault
Seattle
90
Wenatchee
90
97
101
195
Tacoma
Moses Lake
Aberdeen
90
Ritzville
12
Olympia
Ellensburg
Colfax
101
82
7
Centralia
12
Pullman
Raymond
12
Yakima
395
Morton
12
Ilwaco
4
82
Sunnyside
15
5
Pasco
Longview
97
Kennewick
Walla Walla
129
Woodland
Goldendale
14
Vancouver

— WESTERN WASHINGTON —

LEWIS RIVER GOLF COURSE

3209 Lewis River Rd.
Woodland, WA 98674
360-225-8254 $29

We start with an out-of-the-way course in a nice setting along the Lewis River. Short but tough with water and sand. For maximum challenge, play from the back tees and you will experience the 649-yard 12th, the longest hole in the state. One of the better courses in the Mt. St. Helens area.

Directions: From I-5 take Exit 21 and head east on 503 (Lewis River Road) 6 miles to course on your right.

RIVERSIDE COUNTRY CLUB

1451 NW Airport Rd.
Chehalis, WA 98532
360-748-8182 $20

Great rural atmosphere along the Chehalis River. Easily walkable and well-maintained, this course features very quick, rolling greens. Fairways are more forgiving. Nice course and a nice place.

Directions: From I-5 take Exit 79 and head west 1 block. Turn left and follow to course.

TUMWATER VALLEY GOLF COURSE

4661 Tumwater Valley Dr.
Tumwater, WA 98501
360-943-9500 $24

Built in 1968 by the Olympia Brewery on the site of its famous artesian wells, this is a good, solid track with sand and water hazards everywhere. Wide-open fairways, great mountain views and a good practice facility.

Directions: From I-5 take Exit 103 and head south to Custer Way. Turn left and go to Capitol Blvd. Turn right and go to E St. Turn left and follow to course.

CAPITOL CITY GOLF CLUB

5225 Yelm Hwy S.E.
Olympia, WA 98513
360-491-5111 $22

Strong public course located east of town, offering great views of Mt. Rainier and plenty of sand bunkers. Full-service facility regarded as one of the best winter courses in the area due to an excellent drainage system.

Directions: From I-5 heading North take Exit 108 to College St. and turn right. Continue to Yelm Hwy approximately 3 miles. Turn left and follow to course. From I-5 South take Exit 109 and left onto College. Then to Yelm Hwy and the course.

LAKE SPANAWAY GOLF COURSE

15602 Pacific Ave.
Tacoma, WA 98444
206-531-3660 $19

Long and challenging layout in a beautiful parkland. Flat, walkable, well-maintained county course is a good test in the South Sound area.

Directions: From I-5 take Exit 127 (Hwy 512) and head east to Hwy 7 (Pacific Ave). Head south on Pacific approximately 3 miles. Course is on your right

NORTH SHORE GOLF CLUB

4101 North Shore Blvd. NE
Tacoma, WA 98422
360-927-1375 $28

Well-designed, mid-length, rolling course with a good variety of holes in a suburban setting, with nice Mt. Rainier views. Excellent practice facilities, an upscale restaurant and a first-rate pro shop. Very comfortable.

Directions: From I-5 take Exit 142B and head west 5 miles to Nassau Ave. Turn left and continue on to Oakmont. Turn left to North Shore and follow to course.

MADRONA LINKS GOLF COURSE
3604 22nd Ave. NW
Gig Harbor, WA 98335
206-851-5465 $20

This is a great little course tucked away in Gig Harbor. Not long and not that tough, although bunker and tree placement can create problems. Nice all-around facility in a very pleasant setting. Good getaway spot.

Directions: From Hwy 16 just north of the Tacoma Narrows Bridge take Olympia turnoff and head west. Take 1st left (Pt. Fosdick). Go less than a mile to 36th. Turn left and follow to course on your left.

HORSESHOE LAKE GOLF COURSE
15932 Sidney Rd. SW
Port Orchard, WA 98366
206-857-3326 $29

Pretty, hidden gem just south of Port Orchard. Scenic newer course that is improving with age. Tough layout with doglegs, canyons and a rather hilly back nine in a wonderful Kitsap Peninsula setting.

Directions: From Hwy 16 take the Purdy exit and head west to 94th St. Turn right and follow to course.

GOLD MOUNTAIN (Cascade & Olympia)

7263 West Belfair Valley Rd.
Gorst, WA 98337 (Bremerton)
360-674-2363 $24

One of the finest golf complexes in the state. This first-class facility features two Eagle Award winners. The Cascade course and the new Olympic course, which has already received national recognition. Both are exciting, hilly and extremely difficult layouts in a Northwest setting that can only be described as gorgeous. Wel- run and well-maintained and an excellent example of what municipal golf can be. This place is outstanding. A "must play" in the Seattle-Tacoma area.

Directions: From Tacoma take I-5 exit to Hwy 16. Continue on 16 to Hwy 3 just southwest of Bremerton. Head west on Hwy 3 and follow signs to course on West Belfair Valley Rd. From Seattle take the Bremerton Ferry. Once in Bremerton head southwest on Hwy 3 for approximately 3miles. Signs will direct you to course.

LAKELAND VILLAGE GOLF COURSE

E. 300 Old Ranch Rd.
Allyn, WA 98524
360-275-6100 $22

Charming, comfortable resort course in a beautiful setting. Very walkable layout can be difficult with several water hazards and sand traps and a particularly tight back nine. Great golf in a relaxed atmosphere.

Directions: Off Hwy 3 in Allyn take Lakeland Rd. and follow to course. To reach Hwy 3 head west out of Bremerton or east off of Hwy 101 near Shelton.

ALDERBROOK GOLF AND YACHT CLUB

E. 300 Country Club
Union, WA 98592
360-898-2560 $33

Outstanding, scenic resort hideaway set above and overlooking Hood Canal. With the Olympic Mountains in the background, this layout features tight, tree-lined fairways that provide most of the challenge. Wonderful fullservice facility. If you want to get away from it all, this is the place.

Directions: Take Hwy 101 north from Tacoma to Hwy 106. Turn right and follow to Union and the course.

DUNGENESS GOLF AND COUNTRY CLUB

1965 Woodcock Rd.
Sequim, WA 98382
360-683-6344 $25

This is a fun course out on the Olympic Peninsula, noted for its many sand traps including one shaped in the form of a Dungeness crab claw. Good maintenance. Very walkable and pretty. Your best bet in this area.

Directions: Take Hwy 101 to Sequim and turn right at Sequim Ave. Follow 3 miles to Woodcock and turn left. Continue another 3 miles to course on your right.

WEST SEATTLE GOLF COURSE
4470 35th SW
Seattle, WA 98126
206-935-5187 $16

Although this course is not quite up to the level of most of the other courses listed in this chapter, it is your best bet within the city, offering great views of the Seattle skyline and a straight-ahead round of golf. If you need a quick fix and can't get out of town, this is the place.

Directions: From I-5 take exit 163 and head west on the West Seattle Freeway. Follow approximately 2 miles to your first light (35th Ave). Turn left and follow to course which is next to West Seattle Stadium.

KAYAK POINT GOLF COURSE
15711 Marine Dr.
Stanwood, WA 98292
360-652-9676 $30

This stunning, nationally rated jewel is one of the best facilities in the state at any price. A championship lay-out that is long, narrow and demanding. Accuracy off the tee is critical. So is a strong short game as you probably won't be reaching many greens in regulation. A real test in a magnificent setting, with views of the Puget Sound and the Cascades. Bar, restaurant and pro shop are all country club-level operations—a true diamond in the rough.

Directions: From I-5 take Exit 199 to Hwy 528 west. Continue west on Marine Drive approximately 14 miles to course entrance on your right.

AVALON GOLF CLUB

1717 Kelleher Rd.
Burlington, WA 98233
360-757-1900 $33

Everything about this place reflects beauty and tradition. A 27-hole championship course designed by Robert Muir Graves in the hills overlooking picturesque Skagit Valley. A fine crew of caddies. A top-notch clubhouse operation. All in a peaceful, relaxing setting. Great staff. Great golf. Great place.

Directions: From I-5 south of Bellingham take Exit 232 (Cook Road) and head east. Turn left at the light on Old Hwy 99 to Kelleher and follow to the course.

SUDDEN VALLEY

2145 Lake Whatcom Blvd.
Bellingham, WA 98226
360-734-6435 $32

Affordable, resort-style golf at its best. This Ted Robinson designed course is stunning. The flat front nine is set in a meadow along Lake Whatcom while the back nine is hilly and heavily treed. The views and setting are spectacular. Definitely worth a trip.

Directions: From I-5 in Bellingham take Exit 253 and head east on Lakeway Dr. for 10 miles. Course is on your left. (Lakeway Dr. becomes Lake Whatcom Blvd.)

LAKE PADDEN GOLF COURSE

4882 Samish Way
Bellingham, WA 98226
360-738-7400 $23

One of the finest municipals in Western Washington and one of many jewels in this golf-rich Bellingham area. Layout is tight and very woodsy. Maintenance is at the highest level and the setting in a parkland is serene and remote. At $20 max, this is a tremendous value.

Directions: From I-5 northbound take Exit 246 east to Samish Way and follow to course. From I-5 south take Exit 252 to Samish and follow to course.

SHUKSAN GOLF CLUB

1500 E. Axton Rd.
Bellingham, WA 98226
360-398-8888 $34

Dramatic, demanding, newer championship layout. This rolling, links-style course set in the country and surrounded by mountains will challenge you on every hole. Excellent country club-level facilities and staff. Just a wonderful place and already being recognized as one of the finest in the Pacific Northwest.

Directions: From I-5 take Exit 256 on to Meridian (Hwy 539). Head north approximately 4 1/2 miles to Axton. Turn right and follow to course.

HOMESTEAD GOLF & COUNTRY CLUB

115 Homestead Blvd.
Lynden, WA 98264
800-354-1196 $34

Our final stop in this section is yet another new championship layout in the Bellingham area. This beautiful links-style course features the only par 5 in the Northwest with an island green. Adding to the challenge here are several ponds and creeks that are usually hidden. Tough but fair and still maturing. A great facility that will only get better.

Directions: From I-5 take exit 256 to Meridian (Hwy 539) and continue approximately 12 miles to Hwy 549. Turn right and follow to Depot Rd. Turn right and follow to course.

—CENTRAL & EASTERN WASHINGTON—

SKAMANIA LODGE GOLF COURSE

P.O. Box 189
Stevenson, WA 98648
509-427-2541 $35

A beautiful, tree-lines course in the Columbia River Gorge. Not very long but the narrow fairways require accurate shotmaking off the tee if you want to score. Wonderful, relaxing spot located within an up-scale resort. *Note:* Another fine course in the Gorge area and not far from here is Indian Creek GC in Hood River, Oregon. See Oregon chapter for complete listing.

Directions: Approximately 30 miles east of Portland, OR. From Hwy 14 in Washington, proceed to the town of Stevenson and follow signs to the course. From I-84 in Oregon, take the Bridge of the Gods in Cascade Locks to Stevenson. Turn right and follow signs to the resort and course.

CANYON LAKES GOLF COURSE

3700 W. Canyon Lakes Dr.
Kennewick, WA 99337
509-582-3736 $20

Recently upgraded championship layout in very good condition providing all the challenge you could want. Long, links-style course set in the Central Washington desert. This is your best bet in the Tri-Cities area.

Directions: Take Hwy 395 in Kennewick to 27th Ave. Turn east to the course.

LEAVENWORTH GOLF CLUB

9101 Icicle Rd.
Leavenworth, WA 98826
509-548-7267 $20

A terrific course in Icicle Canyon, just west of town. Not long but sand and water can make it difficult. Nice setting amidst the Cascades. The town is unique in that it is an authentic re-creation of a Bavarian village. Worth a trip.

Directions: From Hwy 2 west of town take Icicle Rd. south to course.

KAHLER GLEN GOLF COURSE

20890 Kahler Dr.
Leavenworth, WA 98826
509-763-4025 $25

Charming hideaway carved out of a forest in Lake Wenatchee State Park. Short, narrow course plays tougher than the yardage would indicate. Nice resort feel with great clubhouse.

Directions: From Hwy 2 about 15 miles west of Leavenworth take Lake Wenatchee State Park exit and follow to course.

LAKE CHELAN GOLF COURSE

1501 Golf Course Rd.
Lake Chelan, WA 98816
509-682-5421 $24

Located on a bluff overlooking Lake Chelan, offers great views of the lake and the town. Pretty high-desert layout surrounded by mountains. Wind can come into play. The town itself is in a time warp. Things don't seem to have changed here in decades. Neat place. Fun, old-time resort golf.

Directions: From Hwy 97 take Hwy 150 through town toward Manson. Signs will lead you to the course.

ALTA LAKE GOLF COURSE

Alta Lake Rd.
Pateros, WA 98846
509-923-2359 $18

This is a marvelous hideaway located in remote Alta Lake State Park. Solid links-style course in a canyon with mountain, lake and river views. This uncrowded sleeper is in great shape and very walkable. A comfortable "get away from it all" place.

Directions: Take Hwy 97 to Hwy 153 and follow signs to Alta Lake State Park and course.

INDIAN CANYON GOLF COURSE

W. 4304 West Dr.
Spokane, WA 99204
509-747-5353 $22

This is as good as it gets in municipal golf. This championship, nationally recognized course is one of the 10 best in the state. "The Canyon" plays long and it plays tough, requiring every shot you have. A traditional, hilly layout with tree-lined fairways in outstanding condition. Definitely a "must play" course.

Directions: From I-90 take exit 277 or 277a (Garden Springs) and head north to Sunset Highway. Turn left and follow to Assembly St. Turn right and follow to course.

THE CREEK AT QUALCHAN

301 E. Meadow Lane Rd.
Spokane, WA 99204
509-448-9317 $22

Another fine example of the ongoing commitment to great, affordable golf in the Spokane area. This newer course is a sleeper, not yet fully discovered by the outside world. A dramatic layout dominated by 65 large PGA-type bunkers, and the creek comes into play on several holes. A well-tended course with a great clubhouse and pro shop. Your "country club" in Spokane.

Directions: From I-90 take exit 279 (Hwy 195 South) 3 1/2 miles to Meadow Lane Road. Turn east and follow to course.

HANGMAN VALLEY GOLF COURSE

2210 E. Hangman Valley Rd.
Spokane, WA 99203
509-448-1212 $19

Very pretty, wide-open, long, rambling course with heavily bunkered greens providing extremely challenging golf in a wonderful setting. Great maintenance, great clubhouse, great course.

Directions: From I-90 take exit 279 (Hwy 195 South) for about 4+ miles to Hatch Road exit. Turn left to Hangman Valley Road. Turn right and follow to course.

MEADOWWOOD GOLF COURSE
E. 24501 Valley Way
Liberty Lake, WA 99019
509-255-9539 $20

Our last stop in this section is located between Spokane and Couer D'Alene, Idaho. This highly rated Robert Muir Graves design features a links-style layout that is in immaculate condition. Long, rolling and walkable, this championship course is one of the best in the area.

Directions: Just east of Spokane on I-90 take exit 296 onto Mission for 1 mile to Moliter Rd. and turn right. Continue to Valley Way. Turn left and follow to course.

— EAGLE AWARD WINNERS —

ARIZONA

Antelope Hills (North): Prescott
Emerald Canyon: Parker
Papago: Phoenix
Pueblo del Sol: Sierra Vista
Randolph Park (North):Tucson
Silver Creek: Show Low
TPC of Scottsdale (Desert): Scottsdale

CALIFORNIA

Avila Beach Resort: Avila Beach
Coronado: Coronado
De LeVeaga: Santa Cruz
Fall River Valley: Fall River Mills
Graeagle Meadows: Graeagle
Hesperia: Hesperia
Los Robles: Thousand Oaks
Los Verdes: Rancho Palos Verdes
Morro Bay: Morro Bay
Mountain Meadows: Pomona
Mount Shasta Resort: Mount Shasta
Oakmont: Santa Rosa
Pacific Grove: Pacific Grove
Rancho Park: Los Angeles
Singing Hills: El Cajon
Soule Park: Ojai
Woodcreek: Roseville

HAWAII

Pali: Oahu
Wailua: Kauai
West Loch: Oahu

NEVADA

Eagle Valley (West): Carson City
Rosewood Lakes: Reno
Ruby View: Elko

OREGON

Eastmoreland: Portland
Forest Hills: Cornelius
Heron Lakes (Great Blue): Portland
Meadow Lakes: Prineville
Resort at the Mountain: Welches
Rivers Edge: Bend
Tokatee: Blue River

UTAH

Bountiful Ridge: Bountiful
Eaglewood: North Salt Lake
Hobble Creek: Springville
Homestead: Midway
Park City: Park City
Sky Mountain: Hurricane
Sunbrook: St. George
Valley View: Layton
Wasatch State Park: Midway
Wolf Creek: Eden

WASHINGTON

Alderbrook: Union
Avalon: Burlington
Creek at Qualchan: Spokane
Gold Mountain: Bremerton
Homestead: Lynden
Indian Canyon: Spokane
Kayak Point: Stanwood
Lake Padden: Bellingham
Shuksan: Bellingham

—— COURSE LISTINGS BY STATE ——

Free Newsletter Offer

If you would like to receive a FREE copy of our most recent newsletter, contact:

CIGRA Publications
PO Box 50520
Sparks, NV 89435

Ph: 702-331-7205
Fax 702-331-5150

Order Form

FAX orders: 702-331-5150
Telephone Orders: 702-331-7205
E-mail orders: dps@efn.org
On-Line orders http://www.worldwidewords.com
Postal orders: CIGRA Publications, PO Box 50520 Sparks, NV 89435

PLEASE SEND THE FOLLOWING:

- ❑ 1 (one) copy of "Diamonds in the Rough" @ $12.95
- ❑ 2 (two) copies of "Diamonds in the Rough" @ $20.00
- ❑ 3 or more: call for additional savings

TOTAL AMOUNT __________

Any applicable Sales Tax plus all shipping & handling costs are ***INCLUDED*** *in the prices shown above.*

Company name: ______________________________
Name: ______________________________
Address: ______________________________
City: State: ZIP: ______________________________
Telephone: ______________________________
FAX: ________________ E-Mail: ________________

I understand that I may return any books, for any reason, and receive a full refund.

PAYMENT METHOD

- ❑ Check
- ❑ Credit Card: ❑ Visa ❑ MC ❑ American Express ❑ Discovery

Card# ______________________________
Exp.Date ______________________________
Name on card ______________________________
Phone *(If not listed above)* ______________________________

❑ PLEASE SEND ME A FREE COPY OF YOUR MOST RECENT NEWSLETTER.

CALL AND ORDER NOW

Free Newsletter Offer

If you would like to receive a FREE copy of our most recent newsletter, contact:

Order Form

FAX orders: 702-331-5150
Telephone Orders: 702-331-7205
E-mail orders: dps@efn.org
On-Line orders http://www.worldwidewords.com
Postal orders: CIGRA Publications, PO Box 50520 Sparks, NV 89435

PLEASE SEND THE FOLLOWING:

- ❑ 1 (one) copy of "Diamonds in the Rough" @ $12.95
- ❑ 2 (two) copies of "Diamonds in the Rough" @ $20.00
- ❑ 3 or more: call for additional savings

TOTAL AMOUNT __________

Any applicable Sales Tax plus all shipping & handling costs are ***INCLUDED*** *in the prices shown above.*

Company name: ____________________
Name: ____________________
Address: ____________________
City: State: ZIP: ____________________
Telephone: ____________________
FAX: __________ E-Mail: __________

I understand that I may return any books, for any reason, and receive a full refund.

PAYMENT METHOD

- ❑ Check
- ❑ Credit Card: ❑ Visa ❑ MC ❑ American Express ❑ Discovery

Card# ____________________
Exp.Date ____________________
Name on card ____________________
Phone *(If not listed above)* ____________________

❑ PLEASE SEND ME A FREE COPY OF YOUR MOST RECENT NEWSLETTER.

CALL AND ORDER NOW

Free Newsletter Offer

If you would like to receive a FREE copy of our most recent newsletter, contact:

CIGRA Publications
PO Box 50520
Sparks, NV 89435

Ph: 702-331-7205
Fax 702-331-5150

Order Form

FAX orders: 702-331-5150

Telephone Orders: 702-331-7205

E-mail orders: dps@efn.org

On-Line orders http://www.worldwidewords.com

Postal orders: CIGRA Publications, PO Box 50520 Sparks, NV 89435

PLEASE SEND THE FOLLOWING:

- ❑ 1 (one) copy of "Diamonds in the Rough" @ $12.95
- ❑ 2 (two) copies of "Diamonds in the Rough" @ $20.00
- ❑ 3 or more: call for additional savings

TOTAL AMOUNT ____________

Any applicable Sales Tax plus all shipping & handling costs are ***INCLUDED*** *in the prices shown above.*

Company name: ______________________________

Name: ______________________________

Address: ______________________________

City: State: ZIP: ______________________________

Telephone: ______________________________

FAX: ______________________ E-Mail: ______________________

I understand that I may return any books, for any reason, and receive a full refund.

PAYMENT METHOD

- ❑ Check
- ❑ Credit Card: ❑ Visa ❑ MC ❑ American Express ❑ Discovery

Card# ______________________________

Exp.Date ______________________________

Name on card ______________________________

Phone *(If not listed above)* ______________________________

❑ PLEASE SEND ME A FREE COPY OF YOUR MOST RECENT NEWSLETTER.

CALL AND ORDER NOW